Halves of Me

N. J. Clark

Library of Congress Cataloging-in-Publication Data

Clark, Natalie Jene
Halves of Me / by Natalie Jene Clark
p.   cm.
ISBN: 979-8-218-14884-3
TXu2-324-896
Printed in the U.S.A

Small Acts

Spreading inching warmth
Smooth honey flowing lazy
Unmistakable

Warm blanket wrapped round
Smiles peace and soft colors
Comforting Presence

Smiles spreading fast
Heat rising up within me
Blocking out the cold

Howl

Deep deadly silence
Hazy red glowing embers
Brooding calm victim

Still, cease, dead inside
Jagged flames consume my flesh
Tear stains on the sheets

Salty wounds of life
Withstanding all this torture
Is killing my light

Eerie deadly waves
Predator lurks deep inside
Howling for freedom

Crying begging grief
Worlds torn in half, dying breath
Raw, numb, pleading death

Love

Painting words through images
Forgetting another's flaws

Hoping, waiting, wishing
Observing, lurking, smiles

Bright colors filled with
Sweetness and lost time

Hours and hours and hours
Of words passed back and forth

Indeed I do believe
That this is caring for someone
Above your selfish wants

To lay with them and dream
Of an eternity spent together.

Halves

There is a half of me
That begs to be noticed
It dresses me in dazzling colors
Pleading for attention

It throws insane words past my lips
Waiting for eyes to turn to me
It dyes my hair a blazing red
And fills my eyes with the ocean's hues

The other half wishes to hide
Behind curtains of hair
And the designs of a jacket
Trying to shrink back into dark corners

To be seen would be torture
And isolation death
But there is no place in this world
For someone who hides in the open

Colors

Bright streaks of yellow sunlight
Followed by black drops of blood
Pale ivory skin
And lavender purple vines

Deep grey claws
Trailed by the warmest brown
Beige sidewalks
And blue crystal lakes

The shock of a green leaf
In the midday sun
Countered by the stars' bright orange
That burns with the will to survive

Spots of red appear in my vision
Just before I black out
And a white light fixed above me
Remains cold and calculating

Silence

Screaming endlessly
A hoarse voice in my mind
So loud that I can't hear
No matter how hard I try

There is no escaping it
Once it's begun
It consumes and buries and hides
All your emotions and thought

The hope of saying anything
Anything at all, really
Is washed away slowly
Leaving a raw, bare surface

Upon which no thought can grow
No sustenance provided
To slowly kill your brain
From the inside out

And to avoid this death
Is a constant hourly struggle.

Poison

Veins spiraling and swirling
around green leaves
Stained green with poison
That threatens to choke me

It weaves its way through my being
Tainting both thoughts and movement
A terrible, sickening scent
Veiling all the happiness within

Greedily it sucks all the joy out
Leaving a wrenching, empty feeling
Tearing me this way and that
Blocking all possible places for sunlight

A lethargic, painful liquid flows
Through my veins and out my eyes
Coloring the pillow a horrifying dark red
As the venom kills the warmth I found in love.

Cripple

The panic flurries up
Inside your stomach
Buzzing flies
Rising up your throat

With the final word
A terrible shriek
Comes from the animal inside you
Dying

The tears pour day and night
Constant grief
Never ceasing
Always stabbing

It causes you to swell and bleed.

Slow Down

Every minute passing faster
So fast I'm forgetting my own name
Did I really just do that?
Forgetting my own name.

Was I really just walking?
It felt like I was flying
Trying to catch the time
Running through my fingers

Another second has passed
I forget what I did last
My head is spinning
The floor is spinning

Everything. Just. Stop.

I forget how to count
The numbers rolling by
Faceless people
Begging, come back

How could I let it slip away from me?

I can't trust my own brain
I try to hold it together

With clawed fingers
Not enough, I'm falling

Second, tick, flashback, repeat
Second, tick, flashback, repeat
Second, tick, flashback, repeat
Second, tick, flashback, repeat

I'm living in the past
The future around the corner
Present Nonexistent.
I. Forget. My. Name.

What Summer Brings

Her love was soft rose petals
Caressing and beautiful
She blossomed out to me
Calling me by name

I crooned and stayed by her side
Somehow she figured it was false
The petals began to close in
The thorns rising up as ice.

Over time the leaves hardened
Crimson rose turning to cold grey stone
What happened to the pink hues?
When light had fallen

Menacing glares were all I received
What had gone so wrong?
I thought the petals had opened for me
How could I have been so wrong?

Fallen

Beautiful, beautiful
I would croon to her
I'd sing all night if I could.
I'd even write poetry.

Beautiful, beautiful
The definition of her eyes
Warm darkness streaked with light

Beautiful, beautiful
I say as I sigh.
Her arms wrapped around me
I could not imagine being without.

Beautiful, beautiful
Why won't she believe me?
For to me
All of her is full of beauty.

Beautiful

I have experienced many beautiful things.

I have watched the sunrise every day.

I have observed grass rustled by the wind.

I have stared as colors paraded across the sky.

I have heard the leaves dance on branches.

I have listened as crickets sang in the twilight.

I have witnessed seasons give birth.

I have tasted the salt of the air.

I have slept under an endlessly starry sky.

I have been an audience to nature
And yet you, by far, are the most
Beautiful thing I have found in my life.

Haunt Me

You are not my best friend
You are my only friend

You don't stand next to me in the mirror every day
You are my reflection

You are not the highlight of my day
You are my day

You are not always on my mind
You are my mind

You are not the best part of my life
You are my life

You are not the most beautiful creature in
existence
You are the only creature

You do not have all of my love
You are the very definition of my love.

Falling

You've dipped the world in fire
Tints of orange, blood, sunshine, rust, heat

It's like when the morning fog coats the grass
Nothing clearly visible except the sun
Nothing else matters except the sun
In this case you are the sun

But it doesn't feel like you're falling
It feels like you're sinking up to the clouds
Surrounded by blinding pastel colors
That make up the sun's arrival

You can't possibly leave
For you are the sun.

Trapped

I stand alone in a corner
Across from me sits
An arrow and a bullet
Through which I could run to the door

Would it be worth it to
Become a pin cushion?
Oh but a free pin cushion I would be
Pain is short. Trapped is forever.

Soon I will have to choose
Whispers say the door is handleless
But I hear screams on the other side
As well as singing

Standing here, I am saved from the
Immense pain of a metaphorical bullet
But will I ever experience
A life outside this dreamy cellar?

Hooked

I can't live my life
For it is too unbearable
So instead
I live yours

Don't be offended
Your life is so interesting
I can't tear my eyes away

Every breath
Every flicker
Every smile
Become so precious

I could watch you for hours
With loyal admiration
Fueled by the drug-like
High you give me

Watch

This isn't living
This isn't even survival
It's not the undead
I'm not a ghost

I am merely a wisp of smoke
Traveling among hurricanes
The hurricanes of other peoples' lives
As they pass through their years
I can just sit and watch
For I have no control

Screw You

My vision is hazy
I can't discern shapes
I try, I do
My eyes narrow with focus

Sometimes they flash red
I know that
You know that's
Not what I said

But I'm always the one
With the memory that's faulty
Because you can never be wrong

You don't care about the world
You only care about yourself
You're not doing a good job, either
You self centered psychopath

Starvation

This is more than simple need
Or even addiction
It's much more than want
Above hunger

Is there a word
For when you starve over someone?
More exaggerated than addiction
So much living doesn't matter

I starve for you, my love
You are the only food I know
Replace my blood with your song
Breathe in your eyes instead of air

My eyes are lead
Immovable from you
You try tuning my eyes to water
Making them melt away

Inside the Lines

The world was covered in shadows
Without you, but
When you came
They fled from your light

You cast the shadows out
Gave me a sun to focus on
Before I'd just scribble over the lines
Trying to make them happy again

The lines were so black and trapping
Suffocating the color surrounding them
Thank goodness you came
For you taught me to color in the lines

The black ink drips from the page
Now only color remains on the paper of my heart

I Love You

You're purer than
The freshly grown summer grass
So young and vibrant
Thick with green dye
Dotted with water droplets

You glow more than
When a ruby glaze
Paints the underside
Of grey stone clouds
The perfect sunrise

You remind me of
When the sky is a
Perfect blue, masterly lit
Trimmed with shimmering gold
Accented with splashes of sun

Like the forest
Dense with life
Enveloping you in green
Overwhelming, Embracing, Drowning
So pure and consuming

You Win

My marbles lay scattered
All over the floor
So full of color it's mesmerizing
Lying scattered

I don't gather them up
I sit and stare and smile
Watching and remembering a time
When I had held them close

They left when you came
I did not mind
You can have them
The only thing I want on my mind is you.

Freed

You shattered the ice of my brain

Parted my frozen lips

Gave me a voice, gave me a name

Opened my paralyzed eyes

Thawed my cold humor

You taught me to love again.

Sunrise

Colors are too dull
To ever describe it
Emotions dancing all over

Painted and glowing
Proud and confident

Marching, Parading, Rejoicing
Shouting, Screaming, Laughter
Forever rising, hopes in the sky

Whispers

I glitch around the room
Harsh, jerking movements
Sudden and faster than light

Pause against the walls
Cold and concrete
Breathe heavily, head jerks to the side

Glitch, flicker, twitch
Sit still for days
Eyes frozen

Screaming with my mouth closed
Head shaved, eyes blackened
With blood from my lungs

I collapse into a heap of dust
Ashes stirred by nonexistent wind
The ghost of my mind still haunts me
For I can still hear their whispers.

Best Friend

He never goes very far
Standing next to me
Day after day

He's painted a burning red
Walking in my shadow
Always accessible, faceless

His fists are large
His temper is short
Prone to violence

He's my best friend
And his name is Anger

I Hate Goodbyes

I take back everything I've said
Even the good things
You never should've met me
You don't deserve this

I especially take back the bad things
What a jerk I was
So blind and arrogant
To your pleas

You deserve much better
Than I could ever give you
Don't hurt yourself, please
Kill me instead.

How?

You are the white and purple flowers
In field of lush green
You are the sunlight
Slanting through the forest
You are the trees
On which the sunlight dances
You are so full of light
No one ever guessed the darkness inside.

Words

I am so full of words
But none of them are poetic
"Don't do it."
"It's not worth it."
"You have so much to live for."

I am so full of words
But I've been told to silence them
I'll do it for you
I owe you so much
Just know that I love you

I am so full of words
But I don't know how to comfort you
My arms twitch at my sides
Begging to embrace you
Let me keep you safe.

Distortions

Because when you have a shadow
Images become distorted
Inky darkness spreads over sharp light
Seeing things that aren't there
Hearing whispers that were never uttered

The shadow grows from *your* feet
You struggle to remember it isn't you
You struggle to remember
It doesn't make you double-sided

You tell yourself it isn't part of your brain,
Part of you
They tell you it's a phase
Not a part of your personality
What if it is?
Naturally sad, scared, small, death obsessed
Is your brain depressed or are you depressed?

Stutter

My dreams don't make sense anymore
Just colors sprawled across the floor
The colors of my emotions
When did they become so mixed?

Proud, Joyous, Exalting
Worried, Glancing, Stuttering
Aggressive, Wanting, Loving
Fear, Asking, Caution

I don't want to think about
Blood on your arm
Or pain flickering across your eyes
Silver blades on skin

I will myself to be there
To hold you and keep you safe
But I'm not there.
And I can't stop you.

Tasting Pain

My lips bleed chronically
The air assaults my wounds
For I have tasted pain

You think I have it easy
How much you do not know me
You only know of me

Everything that's hard for you
Is just as hard for me
I've just learned to tune it out

I have simply had to learn more
To stay alive
You know nothing of this

I've endured more pain
I've endured harder pain
To stay alive I must learn

Card Game

I had all the right cards
But I played them all wrong
And I even forgot a few

There were so many rounds
But now the game's over
And you took the table we played on

The cards have turned to ash
Never to be seen again
I weep in the empty air

You took the table
Locked it behind a steel door
Waiting for someone else, not me

You're trying to restart the game
With someone else
But we both know they don't want to.

Drowning

I want to distract myself
I want to forget you
I want to just die...
But all I can think about is the grief

The terrible grief of you leaving
I can deal with the hatred
But not the silence
No, not the silence I drown in

Don't let me die
I want to breathe
Don't let me drown in silence
I can't bear it

Just let me die.

On The Floor

I just need some time, please
To readjust back to life
For my heart is broken

It lies shattered on the ground
All that's left is red streamers
Framed by a cold cement floor
Ripped and torn apart
Rivulets of blood, a dark glossy pond
Limp flesh lying tattered
But the worst part
Is that it's still beating, oh so hopelessly
Still trying to live
Aching for air
Aching for love
Why can't it stop beating?
It would be easier
To leave this grey, half dead survival

Eyes

I don't think they're
Windows to your soul
I think they are your soul
Showing who you truly are
So that you don't have to try

My eyes are worn and tired
They are exhausted from staying open
They wish to close forever.
Rimmed by an ugly red
Rubbed raw and rinsed by tears
Grief has poured from them
One too many times
Tipping me over the edge
They are deep pools, filled with darkness
Unending and ancient

Yet still
They find reason to brighten
To live, to love, to laugh
They find the will to sparkle.

Promise

I can feel the determination
Rising up in me
Like a cold, steel hearted stare
Lips drawn in a tight line
Steadily covering more ground

I will fight to keep my smile
I will fight to keep my eyes open
I will fight to keep blood in my veins
I will fight to keep breath in my lungs
I will fight to keep my life

And be able to call it a life.

No.

I'm not giving up
Through all the tears
And all the stabs
The wrenching of my heart

Through sleepless nights
And aching loss
I still can't give you up

Though my days may be zombie-like
And I'll watch through a grey film
I'm addicted to your light

Through each drop of blood
The slashes on my chest
The grief that tries to choke me
I'm not giving up.

Never

Because that four letter words
The one that starts with an L
And ends with an e
Where the o and the v are caught in between,
It hurts to say now.

It fills my head with memories
It fills my chest with pain
My muscles ache to run to you
Your eyes fill mine with tears
Never again will I love this way

Plummet

Before you, I was okay
Flying in the middle of the flock
Coasting
Taking with ease
The stones they threw at me

Then you came.
You used to fly above me
But the weight of your feathers made you sink
You flew with me
When no one else would

You showed me the air above us
We soared above the cluster of birds
We flipped in the air exalting
I never knew how far we could fly

You helped me find
A whole other sky
Bright with its colors
Loud with its laughter
Beautiful, angelic, perfect

Altogether more.

But then the clouds threw a stone at you

You fell, feathers whistling through the air
I dove down after you–
But it was too late–
You were gone.

You leveled out somewhere
Beneath the flock, struggling to rise
I feel straight into a tree
Ensnared in cruel branches
Separated from the sky

I couldn't get out, I couldn't remember
How to rejoin the flock, or even life
After we'd flown so high
To insult true flight with its
mediocre child; how dare they

I've given up my wings
Torn out all my feathers
Just watching the sky, still
It's nice here, low to the ground
It's nice here, close to death.

Sobbing

Her eyes were breathtaking today
Paralyzed with unshed tears
They shocked me and my jaw dropped
I couldn't even look away

They froze me to my core
My eyes were ice, unmoveable
A million questions on my tongue,
But it had frozen too.

What had put such a sad look there?
Oh, right. It was me.
I wanted to wrap my arms around her
Protect her from this terrible world

It threw blades at her
And loneliness
And cruel words
And her family
And me.

That look in her eyes
It wrenched my heart from my grasp
And shattered it
Jagged red shards flung across the concrete

I felt like a child
I wanted to run to the door
I wanted to pound on it
With small, weak fists
Oh so weakly
I wanted to sob and scream
Just
Sob
Sob
Sob
Let the tears drown my brain, my love

Beg beg beg beg beg
Just release her, please!
Make those eyes warm again
Take her tears and make them mine
Don't let her suffer

I wanted to crumple,
A sobbing heap, a mess of tears
At the foot of that wooden door
And beg them to save her.

Fading

She haunts my dreams
The prison where I sleep

Just wisps of air
But I see her all too clearly.

Why does she torture me so?
The silence I drown in

I may be trapped, but only because
I'm searching for that free feeling

I may be broken, but only because
I'm searching of that whole feeling

I was once beautiful
But now I am ugly
For the girl of my dreams
Now stalks my nightmares

Foggy Stares

How am I supposed to let you die
In my dreams of broken butterflies
Once they flew
But now they're shattered
Glistening shards of sharp glass

You feel like a ghost now
So very far away
Just empty echos down the hall
Grey dust covering my memories
Your laugh slowly fades away

Stages of Loss

The confusion, the panic, buzzing flies
They bounce inside my skull, all over my mind

The crying, tears all night
Rib cage pressed to the mattress, grief

Silence, death, eyes unmoving
Marching, stillness, no flare of breath

Vulnerable, head tilted to the side
I still love you, eyes begging

Demanding, anger, knives thrown
Merciless, I hate you, cruel words

I'm sorry, I love you, sprouting
I didn't mean it, I take it back, done

Heartbroken, desperate, ripping agony
Screams, clawed fingers, grief

So beautiful, beautiful, beautiful, beautiful
I need you, I need you, You're gone.

Escape

So many unspoken words
Upon my tongue
But I wait to use them
For when I need yours most.

For when living becomes
Far too much to bear
When my tears become a river

For when the knife beside me
Becomes all too friendly
Gleaming on the sheets, inviting

Your words, they save me
My only hope from dying
My only light in this dark mist.

Swirling

My hand's a circus act
Crisscrossed with thin, red
Acrobat tight ropes

Scars the size of elephant ears
Stripes darker than a tiger's
Red ribbons of flesh
All torn up

My mind now sadder than a clown's face
Criss-cross, criss-cross, criss-cross
I've hired more acrobats than I can pay
Camel backs across my skin
bump, bump, bump–the scars

I memorize the paths
Patches around my wrist

Spider Branches

Shadows dance at dusk
Weave a web of ghostly light
Grieving, wilting, tears

Beacon to the lost

Back To School

Fear, caution, scared, tears
Excitement, smiles, laugh, wide eyes
Hands, hesitate, fear

Denial

I hurt you?
There's still a question mark
At the end of that would-be phrase
For I do not understand it yet

How could I have hurt you?
You, so invincible
You, so full of light
You, so full of laughter

Is it even possible for you to cry?
Do you even have tear ducts?
How can you have tear ducts?
I can't imagine you cry.

No, that's silly.
Of course you can't cry.

Lights Out

I stumble forward, catch myself
Grope the empty air
Test the ground, just my toes
Don't trip don't fall

Have you ever tried to turn the light on
When no light switch existed?
Of course not, that's absurd
Instead I feel lost, lost, lost

Ears pricking, I try to catch every sound
Before it hits the ground
Information that might
Become unattainable

I sway and sway, rocking back and forth
Yearning for support
A wall to lean on
A shoulder to cry on

But in a world of sighted people
No walls are there
And they expect you to stand still

World Gone Dark

A push from the side
Was it my left or my right?
I can't tell with all the noises around
Drowning my thoughts

Standing in the empty air
With no wall to clutch
My body sways to the sounds
My mind sways to my thoughts

Static in the speakers
Shouts across the room
Whispering in my ear
Distracted by a door slamming

My thoughts are a stampede
Thunderous and swift
Who said that? What?
I can't hear you above the noise

My ears twitch, grasping
Every sound becomes information
Flowing through my mind
Too fast, too fast, I can't concentrate

The voices mold together

I can't discern who you are
Thump thump thump
Footsteps, crashes, bangs, whispers

I can't seem to get specific words
Just the atmosphere of the room
I can't see your smile but I can hear it
I can't see your tears but I can feel them

Each voice has a color
Did you ever think of that?
Swirling, moving, dance steps
Red, blue, green, orange, yellow

Each object has a smell
Did you ever think of that?
Warm and old
Metallic and sharp

Did you ever stop and try?
to listen to Crickets and Cars
Door slams and street noise
While focusing on a Conversation?

Just Stop

I sit with my head in my hands
Just stop talking
I'm exhausted
You talk too fast, I can't catch up

Why did you choose that lip stick?
Could you brush your teeth
Shave your beard
Trim that mustache

Talk slower, stop slurring
Are you coughing or saying something?
Don't talk while you're chewing!
I can't understand you

This lighting is dim
This air is foggy, my mind is groggy
I can't see your lips
Are they resting or moving?

My eyes are tired
My eyelids are heavy
Talk slower for once
There isn't a rush.

Far

The floor is swaying beneath me
You voice wavers in and out
Just shut it out
Just shut it out

This darkness...
It's familiar—warm, even
But still it is my enemy
The cause of my nightmares

You seem so far away
Though your voice echoes closely in my mind
Stumbling to you
Each distance learned anew

Is the chair really that low?
My fingers fly against the wood
Where's the doorknob?
Who put it that far left?

My feet are hesitant
My words are hesitant
Everything stumbling
To travel in my blind world

Tense

Your words become a bitter snake
That weaves its way through my mind
Sowing anger, hurt, resentment

My glare grows deeper
My fists clench tighter
The only word I know is "whatever"

I feel restless, I need some space
But all I can do is sit and wait
As your words pierce deeper

Why can't you just leave me alone?
But I make no effort to leave
My daydreams are becoming violent

What Was I Thinking?

You can't help me find myself
You don't even know you
I know your favorite color
You can't tell me mine

Why did I think it would work?
You're just a kid
I'm just a kid

And I knew that
Before you fooled the both of us
Pulling me into the warm fog
So comforting and unknown
We weren't supposed to know it yet

And I knew that
Before it clogged my senses
Dragged me under, overdose
Forgot left from right

It'll undoubtedly happen again
Hopefully I'll actually be able to tell

Selfish

You disguised it so well
What you wanted
I thought you wanted me
You wanted you
To use your heart
Just because that's what you wanted

No more.

How Could You?

I was innocent
I was innocent
How could you have taken it?
To speak your vile words
To see the world
With angry red eyes

I didn't realize I was falling
Falling in love
Why is it falling?
Love should not lower you
It should raise you
Make you better

But with you I was falling
I thought it was fine
After all,
It's all we hear now
I'll find a better love.
I will rise with them.

For You

The more oxygen
I pull into my lungs
The faster my heart beats

The more attention you give me
The faster my heart beats
For you.

Sky Dive

You wrought depression
You wrought destruction
You sowed the seeds
For twisting vines of anxiety

I started to care what I wore
I started to want even more
The attention you gave me
It distracted me

My goals flipped
My independence pivoted
I forgot, forgot, forgot
The path I should've been on

It felt so good, so high
Didn't realize how low I would be
When everything crashed
Live wire, film over, repeat

And all because I let you

Upside Down

Because when the floor
Decides to become the ceiling
It's new. It's interesting.
Distracting and beautiful.

The colors shift
Light wavers
Oh so new
Everything seems better

You take for granted what you had
Gave it up in a snap
For new. For interesting.
For distracting and beautiful.

You stopped to smell the roses
Didn't see the thorns
Scratching at your eyes
Blinding your logic

Of course you didn' know.
Neither of you did.

Even Though I Tried

You will never know
Who I really am
You will never know
How I have changed
You will never know
Why I am happy
You will never know
What I am thinking
You will never know
Where to find me

All because
You never listened

When you come back
When you realize
Your mistake

I won't be there
Because you took for granted
The unconditional love
And the time I wasted on you

Go

Go
Just go
I'm done
And you're dead
Dead to me
Sleepwalking
Drained eyes
Limp, tired
Fake smiles
I see right through it
Dead

But, unfortunately,
You'll always be my light

Scrub

Out of my head
Get out
I'm done
Ready to Forget
But I trained my brain
To never forget you
To unconditionally love you
To help, beg, cry
Get out getout; parasite
No more
Maybe if I never saw you again...

But I'm seeing you in 12 hours
After months of dusty echos

And if all goes as planned
I'll be seeing you every day
For the next five years.

I'm Not Shy

I'd rather curl up in a ball
Just stare at the wall
Never answer a call
My dark closet
Rocking back
And forth
Vocal chords rusted
Rust
Quiet whispers
Hiding in my ears
Screaming
Right when I thought they left

Looking at anyone
My eyes tear up
Vocal chords rusted
Rust I'd rather curl up in a ball
And cry myself to sleep.
Again.

Anxiety

The tears
Just seep in
And replace my blood
The sadness
Comes back again
Haunts me once more

Bitten lip
Raw and bloodied
Old habits die hard

Eyes flicker
Jumpy and scared
Warm tears pour freely

Each heartbeat
Do I live?
Or do I die?

For Tonight

Just hold me
Just tonight
It's all I need
I promise

Your arms wrapped around
I almost feel your heartbeat
Almost hear your breath
Almost sense your warmth

Kiss me
Run your fingers through my hair
Hold me close
Never let go

But as the sun rises
Its rays stream through you
Ghost
Just my imagination

Blank

I want to feel it
I do
But I just don't
Not anymore

I want to feel
My eyes across the page
For hours on my bed
But uninterested

I want to feel
The bass in my ears
The songs running in my head
But uninterested

My favorite things
Gone, blank, uninterested
I want to feel, I do
But I just don't

System Crash

When you feel the weight
Of the world's tears
Pressed to your head
When it's too much
And you just lay there
Too much pressure
Too many tears
To even move
Lest you explode
But that's not even an option
To explode, collapse
What a relief
But pressure
Tears
Blank
Lifeless
Weight

Eyes For You

If I'm being honest
I still love you
I still want to hold you
Everytime I hear something funny
My reflex is to tell you
I still think you're beautiful

It's so hard
To find something bad about you
And even if I do
I excuse it
I don't care
It becomes good to me
How will I ever get over you?

Sacrifice

I smile more now
To make you comfortable
I dress normally now
To make you comfortable
I dumb my words down
To help you understand
I compliment you
To make you comfortable

Otherwise
I am alien
Strange, too colorful, mismatch
Hard to understand
Socially inadequate
Cold machine
But only to you

To me,
I am simply me.

I Feel Like A Child

I need to cry against your shirt
Feel your warm embrace
Never let you go
Beg you to stay
There's always tomorrow
Just stay today
Don't go to work Daddy.

I miss you Daddy.

Worry

There is no boundary of crazy
I wouldn't cross
For you.

Because truly
That's what it is
This madness I go through
Everyday
Worrying
For you.

Overwhelmed

I couldn't help but sob
In the joyous glory
Of this newfound revelation

This beautiful, beautiful
Weight upon me
Though I knew
It would not crush me

Stuck up against
The rocks of an ocean
As the waves pulled
In and out
Crashing desires

For I had felt God's love

Your Pain

Because I tried
Every time that you didn't
I tried
Not to hurt you
I tried
To make things work
Most literally
Trying everything I could think of

But you didn't
You gave up early
Blamed it on me
Empty claims
Because everything
Is always my fault

Not now.
For now I see
All you were ever good for
Was hurting yourself.

I won't suffer for your pain.
Any longer.

Laugh

The sky is laughing at me
With its bright colors
Its deep embers
The freeing turquoise
Shimmering golds
Burning oranges
Grinning yellows
Smoky clouds
Purple dragon claws
Calm blues that whisper elegance
All its pale vigor
All its sinking shades

The sky is laughing at me
With its bright colors

Imprinted

Every time I blink
There you are
Imprinted on my eyelids

My ghost
You haunt me

But the moment I start loving you
Is the moment my hope despairs

Invasion

You have invaded my home
My home, my sanctuary
My sanctuary
Is your prison

You know you've gone crazy
When others' prison
Becomes your only
Safe place
The only place to breathe freely
To by myself
You've invaded my home
You've invaded my mind
You've invaded my sanctuary.

Retrain

Because when I love you
I see only the good
I ignore, excuse
All the bad

To get over you
I have to do the opposite.
See only the bad
Ignore, excuse
All the good.

How could I do this?
After months
Of training my brain
To see only good
And love all the bad.

Dissolve

Before,
I was content
In my little isolated hole
With its quiet warmth
Content to be
Loud in my mind

Then you showed me
What I didn't know I wanted
You showed me your reality
Which was a show indeed

All that's left is thorns.

It Was Nice To Pretend.

At the end of the day,
It was nice to pretend.

How many words
Were fake.
How many barriers
In your heart
Was I blind to?
How many symbols
Must you use
To make us guess your mood?
How many secrets
Will no one
Ever know?
How many cuts
Will no one
Ever see?

At the end of the day,
It was nice to pretend.

More

What causes me
To write this poetry
Months after you left?

What causes this
Snake of confusion
To nest in the
Woven threads of my brain
And stain them scarlet.

What causes me
To drink this bitter poison
Clearly labeled
And convince myself
It is sweet?

What causes me
To love you.

Chained

Though I know you are not good for me
I ignore my precious logic
The one that guides my heart

How can I sit here
And call you harmless?
How can I sit here
And call your silence?
Reasonable.

For you are a bitter drink
Yet I have burned off my taste buds
For you
And drink up your precious hate
Your bitter lies
Your bitterness at trust

Mistaken

How could I not fall in love
With those streaking eyes
Dark curtains of hair
The way you run in the hall
That stammering laugh
And my heart is an endless loop

And that was my first mistake.

Out of Reach

That relationship
Though mere weeks
Was a decade in my mind

The hours we talked
The songs
All the words

I thought you were mine.

But baby,
You were never mine to take.

Endless Loop

Just because I love you
Doesn't make you The One

And though I understand this
Reread this
Retrace this
Recite this
Repeat this
Memorize it
My mind's mantra

My mind is an endless loop
The confusion
And my mind is an endless loop

According to My Memory

All the stupid things
The stupid words
I wish I could take back

The fleeting moments
Of embarrassment
Burned in my eye
Though I remind myself
They were not significant to you

The names I shouldn't have called you
The bitten lips and tears

But then again.
You never apologized

Search

But I still can't find you
In the catacombs of my past mind

Who was I before?
What did I wear?
How did I think?
Who did I know?
How did I feel?
Why was I happy?
Why did I cry?
What did I know?

Who was I?
Through grey fog,
I try to remember.

I think the difference was
Before this
The future felt full of possibilities.

Then you came.

Possibility

"Broken" is still the title
I give myself
Maybe just because
I'm used to it
Or still partially am

But I can feel something
Fixed
Inside me.
Not plated in steel
Not guarded or wary
Not untrusting
Not hard and cold

But fixed and more whole
Through knowing
Knowing my heartbreak
And knowing that next time
Can be different.

Just knowing
The possibility of can.

Scar Me

You are my self harm
The scars upon my brain
and heart

The reason I can't
Sleep at night
My anxiety
At knowing I'll see you
My anxiety
At seeing you

My buzzing flies
Rising up my throat

But how so addictive.

Compass

See,
The "true" north
Confused me.

They teach us
South
Is the true north
According to the world

So down I went
Confused with "truth"
A mess of words

But now
Partially healed
My compass needle
Is pointed north.

At last.
This sweet rest.

Senses

I feel you in my breath

I hear you in my laugh

I see you in my smile

I feel you in my heart

I hear you in each beat

I see you in my blood.

I taste you with my soul.

Demon

While my heart seeks
To shed you in good light
My mind knows
Shadows suit you better
Though it does not persuade
The demon of my love

Default

Everytime I
Say something
hear something
do something

There you are
In the back of my brain
Imagination prodding
You haunt me

Why
Must you be my default?

Not Here

Sometimes,
I can't sleep
For the words that
Sprint in my mind
The poems I must write
The emotions I must write

You know what's wrong
With this picture?
You keep me up at night.
And you're not even here.

You keep me up at night
Writing about you.
Yet you haven't been here in months.

Multitasker

I have mastered
Multitasking.

The ability
To do everything I do
And think of you
All the time.

Excuse

"We are children"
Is the only excuse
I can find
To get over you.

It's not working very well.

None Whatsoever

Say it!
Just say it!
Admit
That it's a punishment
Call it what it is
Admit it!
A way to reinstate
Your precious power over me
A way to reinstate your authority

Admit it!
But you won't
Because calling it
A punishment
Makes it all too real for you

And you'll realize
Your "authority" has no power over me.

Dread

I had a dream about you
Last night
You wanted to be
An "us" again
You were in my house
And you kissed me.

I woke up feeling sick
And sleep evaded me
Woke up in
The middle of the night
With a terrible feeling
Why does this dread
Consume me so?

Forgotten Side

I had forgotten
What your eyes looked like
When making direct contact
With mine.

I had grown so used to
Far away glances
The beautiful side view
Of you
Refusing to acknowledge my existence.

Oppression

Did you see me as this
Black oppressive thing?
Who would only reject you?
Who would only hurt you?
Who could not accept you?

Did you see me as
A reason to cut?
A reason to go home and cry?
Something insurmountable?
Big, dark, never able to please?

Because I don't understand
Where this is coming from
For I only wished to help.

Betrayal

How dare you betray my mother like that
Your rusted mind
Is no match for my raw fury
How dare you
How dare you
How could you?
I trusted you
Yet this betrayal
Means nothing to you
How dare you betray my mother
Scathingly I seek your blood
How dare you betray my mother

Stubborn

I will not let this water
Wash away my anger

I will not let this soap
Scrub away my glare

I will not let this steam
Relax my tense muscles

I will not let this shower
Soothe my enraged spirit.

Troubled

I feel troubled
My eyebrows creased
How could the world be so cruel?

How could the world be so cruel?
Yet what reminded me of this?
I already knew it
The world is cruel
Yet why does my brow lower
At this moment?

Statue

Maybe I'm not talking to you
Because I have nothing to say

I can't trust you
To accept my anger
Or any emotion
For that matter

May my silence
Be a mark
Of what I have to say to you.

Too Far

Why
Why
Why
Must I suffer for your pain?
Why must you cut?
Why must I suffer
This torturous endless loop
Of heartbreak
Of anxiety
Tears
Crying
Screams
Wails
Begging

The cracks in my heart
Have grown too deep
Yet still I must care for you so.

Chameleon

I realized
You have always been this way
You self centered chameleon
Bending this way and that
To please other idiots
Like you

Your insensitive commentary
Has always been there
But you tipped me to the edge
Of my furious abyss
I trust you no longer

Addicted

Do you realize
What you're pouring into your body!

It fries your self control
Slurs your words
Ruins your memory
Your tastebuds desperate
Chasing your friends away
Breaking your family's trust
You are ruining your body
Ruining it
You are ruining your mind
Ruining it
It ruins your life

Stains it an ugly green
Yet still you go back for more.

Undeserved Guilt

What am I supposed to do?
Oh what am I supposed to do!

This guilt is tearing up my stomach
This grief pours out my eyes
My arms clench painfully
For I cannot hug you

I am sorry
I am so sorry
I don't know what I'm sorry for
Yet still I apologize
You should be the one apologizing
Yet still I don't care

I am sorry
I am sorry
My tears thick as your blood
I struggle to remember
This isn't my fault
You didn't tell me
I found out
That horrifying red line
Upon your forearm

What I Did Today

You glared at me from across the room
I saw it this time
Once again you broke a rule
But this time I don't like it.

At first you just ignored me
I wasn't sure what happened
Or what you knew
But now I know, since I held your gaze,
That you know what I've done.

I'm not sure how to reply
If you break your second rule
And yell at me
Should I be
Apologetic?
Angry?
Sad?
Strong?
Happy?
Trusting?
Worried?
Nonchalant?
Indifferent?

No.

I will not apologize.

Tried to Protect You

You vicious thing
How dare you wish
How dare you wish
To take me from my peaceful place
And put me in a worried state

How dare I
Care for you so
How dare I
Give you any attention
How dare I
Look you in the face
And remind myself
Of how I tried to protect you

Too Late

When you realize
All that I've done for you
It'll be too late

How I
Cried for you
Excused you
Lied to my parents for you...
Things I have never done
Given up hours
Of my precious health
To try and make you happy
When your trust was limited
And I naïve to your please
And I naïve to your lies
When you said you would never lie to me
How I
Trusted other people to make you okay
Damaging our relationship
Just to save you, only you

When you realize
All that I've done
How true a friend I was
How truly I cared for you
I will have moved on.

Long Before

I am sorry
But my trust was broken
Long before
You could fix it.

Revenge

What did he say to you
For I will have my revenge

My Confusion

My confusion
My head tilted to the side

You've broken the only rule
I've known for certain
My only ground
On which I could stably stand
You broke it
After months of silence

You made direct contact with me
And now I stand
Completely in shock
My mind screaming questions
My face unforgivably blank
Almost empty while you fill me up

Their Stupidity

A world without electricity
Is quiet
It is quiet
And confused
For we have become far too attached
To our precious technologies

Without the light
They don't know what to do
In the dark
They don't know what to do
Without text on a screen
They don't know how to interact
With other human beings

I say "they"
For I am not included in their stupidity

Brittle

Sometimes
I don't understand
When your eyes seem to say
"All trace of anybody was gone"

Sometimes
I don't understand
When I try to help your tired eyes
Open them to possibilities
Open them to help
And your eyes seem to say
"You are no longer welcome here"

Sometimes
I don't understand
As you imagine your trust
To be a rubber band
Stretched the slightest inch
And it shall break
Oh so brittle
Is your trust

Amused

All this absolutely perfect timing
Draws up my lips, smiling
How amusing this is
To watch the world help me
Guide you back to love

Yes, It Is

I smile more now
Hum a tune
To let others in
For me to help them
I feel at peace now
Enjoying my work
Still caring for you
But this time
Without tearing up my heart

Then you turn around
And upon your face I see a frown

I smile back
To let you know
From your weakling criticisms
Shall not my negativities grow
Amusing, yes it is
To watch you lie to my face
Amusing, yes it is
To watch you wade in waters of darkness
While I am under a soft light
Offering my hand to keep you from drowning

Only gently, never pressing
To keep you away from my precious

Contradiction

I don't understand
How you haven't spoken to me
In 6 months
Say you'll never talk to me again
And then tell me something small.

So beautifully small.
The best thing to bring up
For you are treating me
Like a normal human being
Not dumping emotions on me
But the weather.
An assignment.
So beautifully small.
So beautifully normal.
The best compliment I've received all day.

But when you look at me
I know not to cross the line
I turn away, ignore you
Then you tell me to stop looking at you.

Your mind.
Is a contradiction in terms.

Reasonable

You do realize
How ridiculous you sound
Don't you?

Because while you call me disgusting
I know any other person
Anywhere
Would see my actions
As perfectly reasonable.

You are alone in your defeat.

Snippets

I feel like I know you so well
That you've become a stranger

I won't let you save me
Ever
I will only save myself.

Our love
Smells like dead leaves

You can't keep them from crying
But you can give them a friend to cry with

Your warped fingers
Clawed around my heart
This is not okay

My problem is
I trust too much
Innocently, like a child

Your problem is
You don't trust at all
Slowly killing yourself

Sway

You are the sunlight
Streaming through the trees
The very leaves of the branches
The sway of a beautiful forest

Slightest Inclination

Cutting, —it's addictive
Everything.
Becomes a reason.

Your dog dies
Another cut
A drop of blood
A scar to keep forever

You were called a name
Another cut
A drop of blood
A scar to keep forever

Today just wasn't as good as yesterday
Another cut
A drop of blood
A scar to keep forever

But soon those drops
Add up
To become a stream
Your skin will thirst for pain
At the slightest inclination.
You will make up reasons
Soon there won't be any.

Just the slightest inclination

Same Blade

How dare you
Cut up your skin
While scarring my heart
With the same blade

Each drop you bleed
You take from me
Each drop of blood
Magnified in my tears

I grit my teeth
And hold back my anger
Reserved for us both
As you cut up your skin
And my heart
With the same blade.

Mightily Wrong

It is interesting
How you can openly accuse me
Of all your wrongdoings
So openly
You try to shoot down my esteem

And isn't it interesting
How you don't even attempt
To persuade another's opinion

And isn't it interesting
How you talk of this to none
Claim you are right
And this is just a guess,
But I assume,
My dear child,
Because you are mightily wrong.

Snippets #2

Pulling me in
Pulling me out
The shadows all around
Mouths agape

You
Are a mouthwatering experience

You are the graffiti
Of my life

rapidly increasing
In fluid succession

I can't know you any better
And so you are a dead end

Sweetheart,
Your lies are tragic.

I find it amusing
That your family can't hold it together
When presented with something new.

Number 100

How dare I attempt to write
A 100th poem for you

The months I have written
100 of my precious poems
Wasted on you

Tragic

You can't even look at me straight in the face
When you lie to me
You hypocrite.

You can't hold it together
When told that you are wrong
Because it's all you ever hear
From everyone around you

Your trust issues are so bad
You can't even admit you have them
For fear
Someone will pray open your heart

Sweetheart,
Your lies are tragic.

Weep

The sky is crying
Drops of blood
From under stony clouds

Its elegant weeping
Is absolutely breathtaking
Dark forests underlining it

While the west is set at
A calm navy
My heart seeks to envelope the ruby skies

Separation Anxiety

You and I
Were meant to be apart
But my heart won't accept it

I try to ignore you
And while my eyes my succeed
My thoughts are at your mercy

I can't help
But be so aware of your presence
My eyes grope the empty air
But I can feel you at my fingertips
Every nerve jumping
Hyperaware of your existence

I try to follow
Your ridiculous rules – I do,
But some remain
As shattered glass
Never to be rewelded

You and I
Were meant to be apart
But my heart won't accept it.

Snippets #3

Ah, poetry—
My final calling

Someday you'll realize
All that I did for you

I should hope
That all I want for you
Is what's best

You took my innocence
I shall get it back

You have become
A figment of my imagination

You are a forbidden topic
In my mind

I have tabooed
Your name

And I was so busy
With my writing
My art
My work

That I forgot to get dressed

Dear Children

I cry for you
Dear children
How can this happen
I don't understand
How has the family become
A grey military line
But worse than that
For they cannot trust each other
To cover their backs
When battling through this life

I cry for you
Dear children
Whose trust was broken
At such a young age
Repair,
A nearly impossible feat

How could this have happened?

Cage

You cover up your naked fear
With such false courage
Such false bravado
As to be a smoky mask

No one sees
Your grief filled tears
Or can even imagine them
For your smoke
Meant to protect
Is a barrier
Fumes to cause your eyes to water
And all those who draw near

No one sees you cry
No one sees how you are treated
No one sees your sensitivity
You've locked yourself in a cage.

Lonely

This kind of depression
Is the absolute worst

I'd rather be angry
I'd rather be crying
I'd rather just have something to do.

But instead I just feel empty
And generally sad
I don't even have the tears to describe it
Just lonely.

Yellow

Quiet with my empty thoughts
Under this old yellow light
The one of my childhood
How I wish I could scrub away
Those ancient summer nights
Yellow faded parchment

The ones where I stay in my chair
For hours at night
Rubbing the faded wood carving
Finding creative ways to sit
After having memorized my seat.

I still can't stand
The glare of soft yellow light.

A Life On It

Because I can feel it
With every fiber in my being
How right this is
How true this is
I can feel it

I don't understand everything yet,
No, certainly not,
But have you ever just felt something
So strong
That you could build a life on it?

Can't Blame Me

I don't know how
I can just freeze up
Oh so suddenly
My jaw gaping open
My mind just blank
As you completely surprise me
So unexpectedly

Gabbling like an idiot
I always manage to say the wrong thing
But then again
I'm so innocent
That you can still surprise me
Have I really said all the wrong things?
Or was I just being me?

Reasons

I will try to be happy
Because so many people
Have it much worse
Than I do

And while it is true
That what I have been through
Is not altogether humane
Certainly not ideal
So many have it worse
And I have reasons to smile

Even As I Watch

You're like the moon and the sunset
On the same half of the sky

Absolutely beautiful
The watercolor pink rose petals
Smeared with lilac
Against pale blue
Clouds dizzyingly perfect
With a pure glowing moon
Striped with grey ashes
The moon is just this perfect orb
Slightly fuzzy
In its magnificent paleness
Impossible to compare
It's refreshing cool silver glass
Against the pastel blushing sunset
A beautiful inferno, against pristine cool trees
I wish I could capture this moment forever
Hold it in my grasp
And though I am no painter
I can still paint with my words

But the moon and the sunset
On the same half of the sky
Makes no sense
And it's already fading fast

Even as I watch
The sky darkens

Listen

Dazzling orange fireflies
Hidden behind
A warm black pine tree
A beautiful flickering sunset

I'm trying to listen
To the moon
What secrets will it tell me?
A beautiful flickering
Iridescent silver flame
Fading in and out
Among a deep navy ocean

Put On A Show

I must admit
There is a certain beauty
In metal
In technology
Electric grains of light
Exact numbers
Headlights on a paved road
Pixels in a screen
But have we forgotten to remember
The magnificent finger painting
Of a child smearing paint on the sky
Making a breathtaking sunset?
Have we burned our eyes out
To ignore such natural magic
And focus on our precious electronics

And the sky is happy to put on a show
For me.

Worth My Fight

Sometimes
I just need to realize
That you aren't worth my fight
And I did all that I could

I can't keep tearing up my heart like this
Leaving it in fleshy tatters
A sorry excuse for scarlet streamers

I can't keep losing my mind like this
Unable to relax
To cry over your agonies
For even just a second

Sometimes
I need to realize
That you aren't worth my fight
And I did all that I could

My Fight

Because if I care about you
I will fight for years
To make sure you are safe

I will stay up all night
To make sure you get the rest you need
I will tell everyone I need to
To make sure you are healthy and happy

Many don't deserve
My fight
But if I feel you are worth it
It will never end

Massive Waste

I mean
This is my work
My art
My time and energy
The sore muscles in my hands
And very fingertips
To write down my thoughts
My observations
All the wonderful things I see
And many of the horrible ones.

And so,
Logically,
Allowing your criticisms
To take root in my heart
Is a massive waste
Of everyone's time.

Snippets #4

You reek
Of sickly perfume

These are my words
Do not harass them

I wake up
With poetry stamped in my mind
Wet with fresh ink

I will tear you apart
There is no way you'll be alive
When I'm done with you

The moment I think I am
It all goes downhill

I will burn you
With my fiery words
I will heal you
With my delicate ones

Master of Small Talk

All you're good at is small talk
I can see it in your eyes
You hide everything real
And leave the rest as a joke

You make people laugh
You make people cry
In a short story
Or rude comment.

They don't know what you feel
And you blame them for it
They don't know what you feel
Because you won't tell them

You're angry with the world
Even though it's your fault

You still have a choice
Even after what he's done to you.

Cross It Out

Just cross out my mouth
A big silver tape X
Fill it with rocks
I don't want to talk

I need to scream
But if I talk the screams will come out
I need to scream
But if I scream I'll talk

I need a hug
So that I won't cry
But if I hug I'll cry
I need to cry

But if I cry I'm weak
I feel so weak
But I can't allow myself to be
Why do I feel this grey fog
I don't even know why
I just need to cry

Argument

If you were smart
You'd realize you can't win an argument

You can't win an argument
Because even if you prove
That you are right—
An unlikely event—
You are still wrong in that you are sowing
Resentment, anger, hurt pride

If you were smart
You'd know this
But you're not
So you continue
To stupidly accuse
Twist around what really happened
Changing your circles
Making them unreadable
I hear that uneasy laugh
Watch as your eyes flicker nervously
And we both know your lie
But I say nothing
For it would be a waste of my precious time
To try and persuade you
You stubborn mule.

Toxic People

I need to cut them out
Just get them out
Before they poison my mind

Their insults
Seep into my skin
Their criticisms
Pour into my ears
I see your lips moving
But all I can hear are my violent urges

I need to cut you out
Before your attacks become mine
I won't let you poison my mind
Eat away all my good words
Consuming all that I do
Decaying all that I say
I won't let you.

Everyone Else's Mess

Basically
In this world
You have to clean up
Everyone else's mess.
You better get used to it
While you still can

Adults
They lie to kids
They teach them
To clean up their own mess
But in the real world,
They'll realize in a few years,
Society is made up
Of the people who make the messes
And those who clean them up.

Home Sick

I hate
That you can still make me cry
Make me run away
Hide in my room like a four year old

I feel
So desperately alone
I want my Daddy

Please
I just want my family
I just want to go home

Crying like a four year old
Alone in my room

Like anyone here
Cares that I cry

Forget

Screw you
Screw you and all your precious lies
The ones you hold so dear
And close to your heart

Screw you
Screw you and the way I care about you
How dare I
Think of you still

Screw you
Screw you and your stupid rules
The ones to put me down
Will only assist my crescendo

Screw you
Screw you and your ghostly image
Wavering in my mind's eye
Just knock me out
And make me forget.

Take Me Away

Mommy
I can't take it anymore
I need to go home
I need you to take me away

I don't want to get used
To crying myself to sleep
Every night
Like I used to

Take me away from this place
This terrible place
The place of my nightmares
The place of my tears

Mommy take me away
I'm so exhausted
Of crying myself to sleep

Snippets #5

A full year of poetry
And yet I have filled up
More than my fair share of journals

I've given up
On trying to befriend you

You don't know me
So don't you dare judge

I wish I could still be
That cold, icy
Assignment crunching machine

It had slipped
From the glassy ice
Of my subconscious

I have run my fingers across
Far softer petals
Than yours
Which are quilted with thorns

Foreign

Is it because
I trusted you with all my insecurities
When you held your lies so close
I, alien
I, foreign
I, strange
For trusting you so completely
For knowing my doubts
For understanding my doubts
And trusting you with them?

Sweetheart,
You are tragic.

Pride

Ah,
What do I have to apologize for?
Your list is overdue
Grown far too long
The writing cramped
Barely legible
Through all your lies
You can't even trust me to be wrong

But I
Am willing to crumple up
That miles-long list
With just one simple word
Yet still your pride stands in the way
Blocking the view of my offer

Expectations

I don't have to be exactly right
All the time
Being exactly right
All the time
Is not a humble way to live

You can't have it both ways
So allow me to choose
For I am my own person
You are not me
You do not own me
You need to realize this
And stop expecting it of me

Your Thorns

I have run my fingers across
Far softer petals
Than yours
Which are quilted with thorns

The curtains over my window
At times they suck in
Begging for release
Attached to the small screen
Separating it from the rest of the world

Other times
They billow out
Swelling with pride
Drawing in my attention
So full of free wind
Free to be apart of my small room
My small world

I'd like to become
My billowing curtains
Create my own place
Become satisfied
For not having the rest of the world
And not brush against your thorns
Quite so often.

Snippets #6

When I
Have nothing left
The fire radiating through my skin
Will keep me warm
And anger
Will keep me going

I was never too young
And I understand many things
Yet all the same not enough
For I had missed out on my childhood

Yet it will strengthen me
All the same

I am still
Trying to be free of you

I'll be seeing you in 12 hours...
That's a scary thought!

There's a time stamp
On my love

Subconscious

That's what it was
Out of a book
Out of a dream
Not reality

How can I still want you
The big question
The mystery
Has yet to be solved

And I still see you
In the sky
In the trees
The sun
And every flower that grows under
Its watchful eye

My room is made up of these colors
And I can barely stand to see them
For your ghostly image
Haunts all these memories
Dipped in bitter paint

My subconscious
Just won't let you go

Snippets #7

I went through
A lot of heartache
Over you
I'd like to be done now.

You make me sick
Someone please come and kill
These rancid butterflies

Sometimes I wish
I'd never read a book
For now I must rediscover
Reality

I forgot that to most
Love and lust are not the same thing

This is a love
That can only grow, sweetheart

I must reason with myself
To get my brain
To give up its secrets

Snippets #8

I don't feel like sharing
Today

I am angry
At the world
Why can't we all
Just have the same standards?

I hate you
I hate you with the very pit of my soul

You're going to hell
And I'm not letting you
Drag me down with you

I can't keep sobbing
Like this
Forever

I should've gotten over you
Such a very long time ago

Snippets #9

Sometimes
You're all I can think about
And I hate it

My dream:
That you will never go through
What I did

My trust
Is not easily broken

I had forgotten
How stupid I thought relationships were

I am done
With your foolish blabbering
Get away from me

You really,
Truly
Suck
You know that?

Selfish

You don't tell me to wear
My seatbelt in the car
So I won't get hurt.

You tell me that
So you don't have to pay my medical bill

Would She?

You might think she's better
In every possible way
Funnier
Smarter
Cuter
Easier to be around
Easier to love

But tell me this—
Would she write poetry for you?

Imagery

Dumped the dust of the casket
Billowing clouds of grey
Stirred into cement colored sky
Streaks and trails
Of this grey dirt

Snippets #10

We both have a lot to learn
From our mistakes
Mine was loving you

I look pretty good
For having cried myself to sleep

I will always have the last laugh
Because I won't be there to hear yours

I'm just not good
At letting people go

You are,
Of course,
Of the devil.

You are
My best muse

You are my best muse
And my proof?
139 of my poems
Devoted to you

In Shock

My heart is beating so fast
That it's galloping away from me
And I can still here that
Drum beat
So rapid

But without my heart
I am paralyzed

You Fool

Look at my tears
Look at them
Look at them, you fool
Deal with your guilt
I want you to suffer
Watch them slide down my cheeks
Watch them
Look at what you've done
This masterpiece of grief
Look at it
Stare
I dare you
I will not wipe them away
You will watch them
And you will suffer

Coveted

You are a fool
Your lies reek in your breath
Your eyes betray you
You cannot beat me down
As you wish to
Though I may cry now
In the presence
Of your foolishness
You should like to know
You may read my journal
I give you my permission
With a smile
Read of your cruelties
Once I have published
Each and every one
Of my coveted entries

You May

Oh you realize,
Dear Father,
You may read
All my journals.
You may take a look
Into my haunted memory.

You may stand accused
Of all that I write of you,
Yes you may.
You may read
All my fantasies
Of how I will handicap you
Leave you blind,
Suffering,
Careerless,
Unlovable,
And ultimately
Vulnerable.

As you always feel.

Real You

You know
I may guard my thoughts now
But only so the rest of the world
Has the chance to read them
When you do.

It has always been the plan
For you to read this.
To know my fury
See as it grows stronger.

All your abuse
All your neglect
You may know it
When the rest of the world
Has the privilege
To meet the real you.

Smoke

Before you ever have the chance
To hand my humanity
To my abuser,
Dear judge,
I will burn it
Under your sorry face.

I will force you to
Inhale the smoke
Of lost art
Clog with pores
With my brains' ashes

Never Met

You have never even considered
Laying eyes on my face
And lending ear to my voice

A sorry judge you are
To have never met
What you are judging.

Dart

Shock waves through my stomach
Tides in and out
Of nervous buzzing flies
I don't hear them but I can feel them

My eyes dart around
That's what it is, darting
Muscles tensed
Prepared to run
Prepared to fly
Prepared to fight

My anxiety
Its roots grow from you
Poisoned and crippling
Blackened and charred
I hate you
I hate you
My hands tremble
With anger and nerves

I'm afraid that tonight
I'll be crying myself to sleep

Grey Dead Line

There may have been a time
When I cried for you
But certainly not now.

After mere minutes
Of your cruel words
Flying daggers
You broke my trust.
I don't see how you can regain it.
I don't even care if you do,
Don't even want you to
You're a grey dead line
A taut tether
Loose after a final cut
I just shake my head
I don't see a way
How you can get back to me

There may have been a time
When I cried for you
But certainly not now.

Snarl

You disgust me
You addicts
Letting it control your life
A slave to your desire
Still you pretend you have power

How can you live like this?
Separated from your freedom
You turn away
Trying to ignore the effects
Of the trap you've created

I am disgusted
No other way to put it
I don't even want to help you
You did this to yourself
I step back with surrendering hands
Lips curled back, snarling

Nice.

You'll never guess
What I did today.
I smiled and laughed
I talked and screamed
I danced and ran
I made friends
I did my work
I played music
I had fun
I tried something new
I did something different

I had every reason
To be happy today
All my satisfactions met

Ah, this is nice.

Share

To me
My work is hidden talent
My happy little secret
My own little sanctuary

And this is because
I feel no one would care.
At least
No one who gets my art
My writing
Like I do
And like other writers do.
Not even readers do

I will share my writing with you
The writers I know
Because I am sure
None of you will disappoint me.

Mere Moments

It's peculiar how
Everything
Can become nothing
In mere moments

It's puzzling how
I could've let you
Shred apart my heart
In a matter of seconds

It's strange how
I had leg myself forget
Every sensible thing I knew
Over the course of our relationship

It's regrettable how
I let you feed me those lies
And not even recognize them
As we both began to drown.

Those Times

Even though I couldn't hear them
I could see
All those times
You silently judged me.

With a single look
A stretched out glance
A flicker of thought in your mind
And a change in the subject of our conversation.

I could see it
Your quiet observations
As you thought I was weird
Or acted inappropriately
Stocking these judgments up
Until they boiled overwhelmingly
Foaming over onto a burning stove.

Even though I couldn't hear them
I could see
All those times
You silently judged me.

Laugh At You

Now I can sit here
And laugh at the both of you
Oh how perfect this is
How perfect you are for each other
With all your miscommunication
And unforgiveness
Self esteem issues
Sitting quietly in the back of the classroom
But I know you're loud with your thoughts

I don't have to be sad
Not one bit
Watching how stupid this is
Watch it play out
And end terribly—
Or even better—
Not care at all
Not bother to watch your mistakes
And be happy
Content with my dozens of friends
When all you feel you have
Is each other

Past Tense

You inspired
Some great poetry
Please take notice
Of my past tense

I can't want you anymore
—I can't
But I looked at you
And overwhelming desire
Completely engulfed my mind

No
No
Not anymore
I turned away quickly
But the image of your lips
Is burned in my eyelids still

Little Kid

I just want
To be a little kid again
Bring back my Good Words
And dance around happily
In my weird outfits and colors
Humming to myself
An immovable smile
Not a care in the world

I'm still trying to find
That small child inside of me
And I know I can do it
I know it.

Adjectives

Your words
Say a lot more
About you
Than they ever could
About me.

The adjectives
You use to describe me
Make no sense
As we witness your anger
And my willingness to walk away
From something that has the potential
To become rather violent

Dazed

Your voice is wavering in my ears
I'm sorry, what did you say?
I'm dazingly overwhelmed

Everything is blurred
My actions speeding ahead of me
Too quick to comprehend
Yet all the same
Far too slow,
Or maybe someone pressed rewind

Sometimes
I catch a glimpse of myself
The way others see me
And it's hard to compare to
That other person in the mirror

Everything's in a blender
I'm hyperventilating
Yet only taking in
The slightest drizzle of oxygen
And then suddenly
My lungs collapse inside my chest.
What a shock.

Progressive Status

I'm still working on
Cutting all of you out
Of my life

I'm still working on
Putting myself back together
Chopped up puzzle pieces

I'm still working on
Turning away from her
I don't need to be jealousy stricken

I'm still working on
Drawing closer to God
Who gives me my every day

I'm still working on
So many things
But at least I have something to do.

Slightly Tarnished

My deserved pride
Bright and shiny silver
Newly polished
And yet slightly tarnished
How can this be?

For overshadowing this joyous memory
I hear your tauntings
Your ridicules
Trying to put me down
After I have risen above you
And rightfully so
As I have worked for it
And I have not even provoked
This uncalled for mockery

Tango

I wish I could waltz through this life
Unharmed
But I can't
And so I will tango.

You may see me
In all my dazzling colors
And think how odd I am
But do you take the time
To understand my motive?
No. You don't.
So why should you call me odd?

I wish I could waltz through this life
Unharmed
But I can't
And so I will tango.

Misery Loves Company

Ah and misery loves company
Soaking through the fibers of your being
Staining it a deep scarlet
A lovely color
But fatally dangerous

Ah and misery loves company
I marvel at how you can stand it
To throw your hatred
At everything that crosses your path
Indeed I marvel

Ah and misery loves company
For it is such a lonely state
And I will not join you
Though you attempted to drag me in
I will not sit and be lonely with you.

Let Go

It's tragic
How I have to explain to you
Why I saved you

I shouldn't have to confess
For I did nothing wrong

And even after that
Sometimes you just have to let go

Favorite Color

No one even knows
Why my favorite color is black
I love this
Because it means heat
Chaos
Bodies pressed together
Close spaces
Endless interchanging night

And in the day
Everything is cast under a stark light
There is no room for colors to shift
Everything cloaked in black
Has the potential to shift in and out

Black is when people draw together
The darkest times
Are when we pull together
And create armies
Fighting battles side by side
The darkest times
Are the closest times.

And to be even franker
I look wonderful in black.
So don't call my antisocial

You're not even using it right
And I think much deeper.

High School

We are children
I watch as your thoughts flare up
Furious red flames
Automatically defensive
You are not adults
You do not do adult things
You'd like to think so
And that's what's wrong with this title
The fact that we are innocent children
Is often seen as demeaning
And so we think
We must grow up too quickly
Yet we are only imposters

You are so angry
Because I am right.

Dumped

I knew it I knew it!
I called it, I knew it!
I saw this coming
You wouldn't let me warn you
I knew the second I found out you were together
That she'd be the one to end it
And poorly ended it would be.

Toll

All the heat is dripping from my fingertips
All that's left is deflated rubber husks
Slow to pick up
Straining all the muscles in my forearms
While the rest of me is full of energy
My hands are useless slugs
Trick or treating
Has taken quite a toll on me

Soft

I can feel her in my soul
Feel her soft breath
Humming against my chest
Quiet and peaceful
Innocently sleeping
Unconsciously pulling closer
Embrace tightening
Only for just a second
Eyes flickering behind closed lids
Dreaming

Click

I shy away
From all those songs
That remind me of you
I shy away
From all those songs
I listened to in my depressed state

They set my heart
On fire
And in a cold sweat
Ice frozen
But still galloping away from me

My eyes dart up
And my thoughts sprint
My head seems to scream
My heart begins to melt
All of me is running away
And I'm still in my seat

Then with the click of a button
The lyrics change
How I wish
I could do that with my memories.

Dart #2

It's primal instinct
That's what it is
This drum beat inside of me
That's why the moment I step in
I'm looking
For all possible forms of escape

It's why my back goes rigid
And my breath speeds up
My muscles are melting
So tensed they've turned soft

It's why I don't utter
A single word
Why I can only dream of moving
And I can't focus on your voice

It's an endless spinning turbine
Of unrelenting restlessness
My body is training
To survive longer than you

Art

Because they have no curiosity
And so they forget
They do not ask questions
And so they do not learn

They tell us we need to grow up
And that wouldn't be a problem
Growing up is not the predicament
Forgetting is

Don't we all agree
That being a child
Is so much better?
So why have we all forgotten?

Art
Is the secret to keeping your childhood

Exist

Ah this music
It causes my heart
To swell and sing
It moves me from my chair
Set my feet aswing
Places a smile
Upon my memory
And I cannot help
But laugh uncontrollably
At how happy I am
At this beautiful music
Almost too beautiful to exist

Dark Recesses

In the dark recesses of my mind
In the dark corners
Lay everything important

Nothing is left
In the forefront
Nothing is there
Nothing save you
And you should be nothing

Still I cannot reorganize
The boxes seem so heavy
And you seem so immovable
Unmalleably strong
Engulfingly invincible

I had forgotten
Your magnificent façade
The word I used to mispronounce
But ah
I still remember the definition
Now to just apply it to you
And place you
In the dark recesses of my mind.

Dim

The lighting is dim
And this is when I triumph
When I move ahead of you
Confidently and practiced

No more stark sunlight
I thrive in the dark
I thrive in the chaos
I thrive among throngs of people

No more stark sunlight
It has slain my imagination
And causes it to run haywire
I cannot focus
Through my veil of fog

But in the darkness I thrive
In the chaos I thrive
Among throngs of people
I do indeed thrive

Oh won't you please
Dim the lights?

Taught

I still don't understand
How you can stand
To live like this

Then I remember
You have been taught
No other way
Than fear
And broken trust

I can still feel you
Feel your heartbeat
Across the room
I still watch over you
Night and day
And we both pretend
That I don't care

But this bond
Won't be broken
I can feel it now
We have peered too deeply
Into one another's lives
To ever forget

Pray

I've been locked in the same room
For nearly 14 years
And sometimes
It really sucks

Sometimes
I wish I could escape.

Sometimes
I wish I could
Be like normal kids.
Unthinking
Playing with toys
Doing such wonderfully
Impractical things

But instead
I think
And I sit
For hours
And I just write
And pray my thoughts
Are not stolen from me.

Ghost

I don't feel
Like looking at a ghost right now

Because that's what you are
To me now
You've slowly
Been disappearing
You're slowly
Becoming a stranger
My eyes
Can hardly focus
On your opaque form
You're just somebody
That I used to know
I don't know you
And trust me, I've tried
With my limited
Information and resources
To watch over you
But I've hit a brick wall

So why
Should I care for you
At the cost of my health?

Twisted

I went back
And reread
How I described you
To all my friends

I can't believe
How drunk I sounded
How drowned I'd become
In the image of you

I described you
As glorious and beautiful
And had ignored
The results of all you'd done to me

All the blood and tears
The pain you put me through
And still
I worshiped you

Now that
Is most definitely twisted

Innocence

Innocent?
Innocent!
Ha!
I should think not!
More innocent than you! Bah!
How could you
Have counted my crimes?
For though yours are many
I have done much

Innocent?
Innocent!
Ha!

Wait
Why do I declare such folly things?
Innocence is good
Innocence is white and pure
So why has society
Twisted our view
To make evil doings
A tragic norm?

Heat

You're still so angry
Your words are infuriated
And fuel an inferno
Only hate can bear to stand
This excessive wretched heat

Every aspect
Of the way you talk and move
Screams at those around you
It's so angry, so angry
Until it foams over

Your burial did not succeed.

And my scars
Can't leave
Ah what a mistake you were

Refuse

I'm sorry
Were you not given
The desired effect
You asked for?

Because I refuse
To curl up into a ball
In the dark corner
And sob

That is not how it works.
If you are cruel
My anger will only grow
And my pillow will remain dry

I am not weak
As you will me to be
Your words cannot penetrate
As I rise above you

6 am

I let you put me
In the worst depression
I've ever been through
In my entire life.

And I would hope
That I would not hesitate
To completely reject
All of you
And anything having to do with you.

Transfixed

My eyes remain transfixed
On the magnificent beauty
Of you

You most literally
Light up my world
And fill my day with paint

Everything is brighter
With you in it
You're a reminder of hope

You guide them to the end
Of the darkest night
And refresh our minds

I love to sit
And watch you every morning
What a great start to my day

By Your Side

I don't know many
Who would stick by your side
When I'm an option

You have proven to them all
That you are quite a pest
Though I would never
Call you that myself
And I stand alone
Of that opinion

Grate

Your voice is grating
On my ears
And I cannot hear
One more moment of it

For you have pierced a nerve
That was never intended to be touched

Metal teeth sink in
On my patience
Oh grate indeed
I clench my jaw
For the love of everything
Just shut up already

Exhausted

I'm so tired
Of caring for you

Why must I feel
This eternal sadness?
Why must I fear
This unquenchable worry?

Tired
Just exhausted
I'd like to fall asleep for once
Instead of all this
Lying awake for hours.

Manacles

While my mind prays
To finally be over you
To finally be free of you
My heart
Is certainly not finished.

It's been chained down
With rusty manacles
To a cold cement floor
And beats weakly
It turns the other way
Claims the only thing to hold it down
Are beaten threads

And sometimes
My heart does feel beaten threads
But others
The chains are heavy upon me
And all too real, cracked silver

Those times
Are when you need to be protected most
And when I am all too happy
To wish I could.

Half-state

It's like I'm fading in and out
Some days my barely solid form
Stands far away from you
As it should be

But others
I fade softly to your side
And watch over you
I cannot help
But wish I could embrace you
And keep the hardships away

I'm just pastel colors
Mostly see-through
I'd like to be solid
On one side or the other
But my heart and my mind
Can never seem to agree
And so I am in a half-state.

Sold

What is the price
Of my health?

For my brain knows
Not to give it away so easily
However my heart
Is a completely different story
It is completely sold on you
Placed all its bets
And I cannot help but wonder
If there's a reason.

Should I even be trying
To escape still?
What will become of this?
What will become of us?

For surely
There is a reason
My heart is oh so entwined in the image of you

Aren't Going Away

You're a book
That I can't put down
Forgive me for staring
But you are easily
The most interesting person I've ever met.

And you may think
You're life is so infinitely boring
But your problems
Puzzle my mind
And I cannot help
But waste all my time
Searching for a nonexistent solution.

I wish
I could stop thinking
And stop being in the right places
And all the right times
When others are spewing information on your
whereabouts

I can't want to know anymore.
But these scars
Aren't going away
And neither are you.

Stopped Crying

Yes
It was sad
That we ended
But I've since stopped crying.

A final chord
A striking blow
The last cut
A bucket of tears to follow
Suddenly
All I have to walk next to
Is empty air
You're irreplaceable
But it seems
The air didn't get that message.
While you seem to be
Grey dead dust outside
You are mightily alive
In my heart and mind.

I still feel a rope between us
But I have no idea
Why it remains

Yes
It was sad

That we ended
But I've since stopped crying.

Disagree

My mind knows
You're not my responsibility
So why must my heart disagree?

My mind knows
You don't need protecting
So why must my heart disagree?

My mind knows
You don't need me
So why must my heart disagree?

My mind knows
I shouldn't care for you still
Oh, my heart! —disagree indeed!

However my mind
Also knows
That *they* do not do as they should.
They do not take responsibility
They do not protect
They do not need you
And I should hardly think they care!

And so my heart feels it must.

My Words

To me
These pages are full of at
While it might seem
They are only made of grey pencil streaks
To me
They are full of wondrous color

They curve and twist
With sharp edges
All my words
—For they *are* mine—
Pull together
In a wondrous array

These pages are mine
These words and thoughts are mine
And they are beautiful to me.

Sliced.

You can try
But as much as you wish
I can never let you
Beat me down

It just doesn't work like that.
For while I am full of sunshine
Your dark clouds
Have no effect on me.

If anything
My rays slice through you
And I cut you
Into a thousand streaming pixels
My happiness
Splits up your darkness
And banishes the dust
I spread
And do not spread thin
There is enough happiness
For everyone to partake of.

And you.
Can't stop me.

Grey Fog

I was just
So grey that day

And not the good kind of grey
The closeness that I love

But the drowning kind.
Where my smile melts away from me
And does not float back.
Where no matter how hard I try
The fog won't leave
The fog won't leave me
It just won't

Where you're the only thing that matters
The only thing I can relate to
The only thing I can talk about
The only thing I can think about
The only thing I can cry about

And I suffer
I bleed for you
But still
It does no one any good.
And I keep drowning in the grey fog.

Runs Red

Seeing those scars
Just imagining
Seeing those scars
Drives me absolutely insane.

It draws me to action
And my throat aches
To scream at him
And my fists ache
To pound even an ounce
Of decency into him

All that he put you through
I wish to put him through.
I want to thrust my dagger in
Oh so deep
And twist
And twist
Till the last thing he sees
Is my raw fury

How can he do this to you?
But I stay in my place.
While my vision runs red.

Heart Rotted

Because I can see the pain inside
While they are too afraid to peer in
And see what the world is made of
See what the world makes of us

I so desperately
Wish there was more I could do
But while they remain as statues
My resources are limited
And I hate them
I hate them
For letting your heart rot
The love that should be for yourself
Is nonexistent
And I can hardly express
My fury over their
Inability to be decent human beings

Seeing Stars

My world is spinning
My heart is spinning
And I'm standing in the middle of it all

A world is just so
—Empty,
Without you.

It's as if
All the stars were sucked out of the sky
And fell in love with your eyes

Resurface

Because when I look at you
You are unearthly.
So foreignly beautiful
I can hardly stand
To look away.
I want to drown in you
For a couple eternities
And never resurface
From your beautiful dark colors

But when you look at me
I see you as you really are
A girl
Just a girl
Struggling to find yourself
Your eyes are a bit warmer
When faced head on
And suddenly
Overcoming the challenge of getting over you
Seems a little less impossible.

Emptier

Sometimes
I am utterly disappointed
In myself
When I react to your absence

When suddenly
The world seems emptier
And my eyes seem to grey
And I can't help but stare
At where you should've been

I shouldn't worry anymore
But my heart will never listen

Body

You disgusting fool
How could you
This is my body

Changing

I don't know why you insist
On making me the bad guy
But I can assure you
It won't work.

I've tried too hard to change
For anyone to think
I could possibly sink as low
As you claim I have.

Foul

The insulting words
You choose to throw at me
Only insult you
And your integrity.

They prove
How foul your tongue is
And do not persuade
My heart and logic.

Save It Be

I should hope I would not
Glimpse your father's face
Tonight
Lest no one ever sees it again

Ah
And the trouble of your world
They do indeed disturb me
Quite mystifying, yes they are

And how should I ever have hoped
That you would look for help
On your own?
For it is by a leash
That I must drag you along
Out of these situations
Most of them
Magnified in your accusations

I think you insist
On making me the bad guy
For you have no one else to blame
Save it be yourself.

How Little Time

Ah and I had not realized
How little time we have
For it is but a moment
That makes up a man's life

Then how long,
Pray tell,
Should our worlds
Fall in place?

How long
Do we have
Before we are split?
Torn paper

How little time
I have with you
And I will not waste it
No—
I will do what I came to do.

Motion

I have closed your door
And opened my window
For sunshine comes
From open windows
How could I possibly think
They came from your hall?

I took this opportunity
To change
You see.
Mistakes are solid proof
That I am trying
Yes
I make mistakes

You claim
That I was a mistake
So why not take a knee
And learn from it?

Apology Unaccepted

And when have I
Refused to apologize?
Every time you accuse me
Let it be big or small
I have taken full responsibility
No matter how ludicrous your claim

And when have I
Ever dreamed of having
Any small utterance
Of godly sorrow
From you?

None!
So now that you have no reason
To reasonably accuse me
You call a fraud to my apologies
And so who will be sorry
At the last day?

Oh
Certainly *not* me!

Bitter Paint

Oh!
This bitter paint
That thins my blood
I did not turn away
Quickly enough!

Oh my heart!
I feel this sting
Why was I there!
Why did I look!
Oh why must I know
These retched details!

And ah my ears
These words fall upon
Cold grey statues
But, no
No
I must call upon my sunshine.

Retched Sorrow

Ah, yes
Bitter
For that is what I am
After these months of turning away
How could I have looked once more!

This sorrow
This retched sorrow
Leave me be!—
My demon
My grey fog veil

I will not let you drown
More of my optimism
And ah, yes
Optimism does float
Does it not?
So why must it
Endure these cumbersome waves!

Troughs

And these waves
Troublesome they may be
I long for the crest
Upon which sunshine flickers
Oh beloved sunshine

But the troughs
Ah the troughs
I look down upon you
As you swallow me up
Cold shadows
Inevitably
Yet I struggle to find my crest
Once more

I long for
Calm clear glass
A settled ocean
To travel upon

But with you
I am a troubled sea
A sea of tears
Salt in my chests' slashes

Imposter

Oh the flame you lit!
The match you threw!
The irreparable burns of premature love
I suffer now

Why must these children
Insist on growing up?
For far too fast
Is their flight from childhood
A sudden blur
Of bright colors
Now replaced
With grey confusion

How could you
Want to become an imposter?
For that is what you are.
A fake
And an indecent one at that.
You're not even growing up
The right way.

Fun House Mirrors

Oh yes
I can paint quite a picture
For the truth is my ally
Would you care
To spare me your denial
And accept reality?

For I am not the enemy
You
Are your greatest enemy
I am not the cause of your sin
You are the only one
Who can control that

I see you
Attempt to contort my image
Fun house mirrors
But carnivals,
My dear,
Don't last forever.

The truth
Will come out.
I can be certain of that.

Crushing Responsibility

And who is to decide
My fate?
You?
Oh I should hope not!
The weight of that
Kind of responsibility
Would certainly crush you!

You are no god
And don't mistake my words
For I believe you have potential
But my dear
Our judge waits above
And you are down here

Spare your time
Spare your energy
When it comes down to it
Only your pride will be hurt
And I should like to think
My slate would be rather clean.

Oh Your Pride!

As fate would have it
I am rather stuck to you
And may I remind you
—Ha!—
You planned it, my dear!

This is no fault of mine!
Oh I need a moment!
Excuse my laughter
But how twisted
This really is!

That your previous judgment
Of my past character
Should be your very demise!
And even as I try to save you!
You still insist on drowning!

Ha!
Oh your pride
Would be the end of you!
And prove myself
Just still!

Deception

Truly,
Torture?
Ha!
I must laugh at that!

Where do these
Ludicrous ideas
Come from
Might I ask?

The deepest pit of lies
Yes, that seems a timely match
You dug so far down
That no one can quite believe you!

You cannot even deceive your friends!
Ah what an alibi you have
Your closest acquaintances
Have sided with me once more!

Shift

Uncertainty!
What a demon it is
What a black pesky fly
Buzzing around my mind

Do not enter my heart
I warn you
For I might have to
Burn you out

Sprinting

Anxiety
It runs through my veins
Or rather sprints
What a sprint it is
For survival
A threat unbeknownst to me
My senses have seen
But a dark shadow
Is apparent in my mind
Yet still I must flee!

And what questions
Hang about my mind
However there is no time!
I must spend my day in a blurred race!

Leapt

Oh and my heart
Leaps!
At the sight of you
How dare my heart
Jump!
At the flicker of your eyes
Sliding across mine

And in shock
I cannot form a reply
At the state of your
Rather random commentary

Your attacks
Only give me to opportunity
To prove myself as better
And stronger still

I dreamed that I was burning.

Every inch of my being was dipped in orange fire.

I writhed painfully in my sheets for hours before I finally came to.

When I woke I could still feel the pricks and stabs of the torturous flames.

I bolted upright, and felt an impossible chill wash over me, my lips the coldest. My eyes were met with darkness.

I blinked, but to no avail.

The image of engulfing black remained the same.

Locked

My secrets
Locked against my chest
You will not pry them from me
Yes I can assure you of that!

For while I am full of words today
They are out to get me

Sunset Today

Charcoal scraped across the sky
Laid against pink hues
Set against the blue softness
Streaked against yellow rays
Rival to the orange flames
Accomplice to the purple flowers

All working to out perform
The pale white sheet
Of the glowing moon
Gazing down
On our dark bare forests

Lost Sight

The image of you
Caused me to lose sight
Of how truly amazing I can be.

Truth

The truth *will* come out
There is no use denying it
It *will* be known

There is no use delaying it
It *will* be known

There is no use in hiding
It *will* be known

There is no use in lying
It *will* be known

You see the truth
Demands to be seen
It demands
To set things straight

And you, my dear,
Are certainly not straight!

Rather Blue

Ah, I see now
You demand that your opinion
Be fact.

But ah
Your opinion
Is not fact.
Your opinion
Does not change fact.

And as hard as you may try
To convince everyone
That the sky is red,
It still looks rather blue to me.

Snapped Back

I didn't sense how
Your fakeness
Had come to turn my life

Alas my heart
Had begun to turn to plastic
I didn't even feel it
Didn't even feel how wrong this was
The child in me
Knew which way was north
But then I tried to grow up too fast
With you

The taut rubber band
Snapped me back
Into reality
I'd stretched myself too thin
Oh far too thin

But now I truly see
Your demented faking
Ah, you compliment me
For I do lack, you are quite right

I can never possibly be
As fake as you are.

Vile

You don't understand what I'm saying
Because you've put a cup over my mouth
Empty echos

You would understand my words
If only you tried
But you've chosen to trust a lie

I won't dumb myself down for you
No, never
If my words are too long for you
Don't bother wasting your time

If we are to communicate
It will be on my terms
No more
Of your vile profanity

Shadow

Shut up shut up
Get away from me
I truly don't need to think of that
It'll to me no good
To reinstate
My grey fog veil

For with you
My veil is permanent
And I can hardly wish to focus
On anything of true importance

I cannot allow you
To distract me any longer
I must turn away
For I have found
That you do not cast out the shadows
You are a shadow in disguise

Only sunlight
Casts out all shadows
I cannot take your dim static
Any longer

Weekend

Oh and what a marvelous time!
I had without you!

No second thought to your opinion
No ridiculous pondering

I could focus on reality
And not your ghostly form
A much needed break

I did not bother myself
With worrisome thoughts
No more grey veil
No more cumbersome waves

Alas
Only a weekend

Foul #2

But your mouth
Is still as foul as ever
And I had thought
Maybe you had changed
Alas
I was wrong

From you
I have come to understand
I cannot save those
Who still insist on drowning
My dear!—
But what a mouth you have!
How can these children
Bear to stand near you
Truly I do not
Understand how
Any can possibly tolerate this

Sick

It makes me sick
To think that children
Could possibly do something
So completely horrible
And certainly not ordained of God.

Yet still I have hope for you.

December 4, 2017

If you remember all
That you have

You'll forget about
All that you lost

Attention

You wish for my attention
But my dear!
You have stayed it!
No attention of mine
Shall ever be given to you again

The more you ignore me
The more I look for you
How utterly ashamed
I am in myself

The more I ignore you
The more you look for me
So many questions
Racing around my mind

Ah this circle
Conversation of glances
Not only words
But feelings passed as well.

Dismay

I am quite dismayed
With your profanity
For if I had a mouth
Half as rotten as yours
I should be utterly ashamed

How can a child
Declare such vile things
This profanity
We hear such things
All too often

And even so
Your tongue is the most ludicrous
I have heard of the lot!

Too Loud

Ah and do you know why
I turn away from you?

Of course not!
Your blabbering tongue
Remains too loud
For you to listen to me!

Appreciate

I don't appreciate
Your criticisms
And thoughtlessness

And the way you attempt
To drive the dagger in
But to no avail.

Your manipulations
Can penetrate me no longer

Mistaken

I'm afraid you are mistaken!

And your pride
Your denial
I can tell you now realize
How very wrong you are
And still!
You will not admit it!

Trust

If your trust
Can be broken so easily
It's honestly not worth having

I'd rather live in peace
and comfort
Than spend my days worrying
About what you think

If your trust
Can be broken so easily
It's honestly not worth having.

Way To Live

And how else should I
Go about "getting over you"?
Do you expect me
To get up one day and say,
"I'm never looking at her again"?

Now that is a fate
I wouldn't hope to wish upon anyone
What an
Uncompassionate way to live

Real Love

Real love
Shouldn't tear you down
And take things from you
And cost you your health
And steal your happiness
Make you desperate
And certainly blind!

And how should I
Have expected anything more?

From people who
Have absolutely no idea what we're doing
From people who
Are trying to grow up far too fast
From people who
Have given up on looking for themselves
And learn someone else instead

Tested.

Of course I knew
Close to nothing at that time.

People like to say
That I'm smart
But truly
If you tested me
I would certainly fail

Of course I didn't get you!
How could anyone!
If you don't let anyone in,
How do you expect them to know you?
And then you blame us!
For your trust issues
You try
To make me guilt-stricken
I can assure you
That now
I have learned much better
Than to give in
To your selfish
And rather stupid
Accusations

Sorrow

You may demand
Sorrow from me
But truly
I am not full of sorrow today!

The most I can say of you
Is that I have grown
From the trials I let you put me through

Remember

I want to help myself remember
Right now.
How I feel
Right now.

How completely convinced I am
Of how happy I am
And how long
I know this can last
It doesn't seem like hard times
Are anywhere near me
But just in case

I want to help myself remember
How happy I know I am
And how happy I know I can be.

Someday

I went through
Far too much pain
Trying to save you
And frankly
I'm about done

I tried
Literally everything
I could think of
And now I'm out of ideas

I just pray
That someday
You'll realize how much I cared for you
And know
That you are very much worth loving.

Just Trip.

Falling into love
What an easy feat
Just trip
—Just forget—
And you're there

It's easier to drown
Than to tread water
Especially when you don't see
The mile high waves in the distance
And the thunder clouds
Growing overhead

Now to rise
How difficult!
To rise out of love!
I've hardly heard of such a thing
Now that I've fallen
So completely
My heart wishes to stay on the ground.

Ignorance

I am quite puzzled
With the way you talk
To your own friends.

I hear such rude words
Passed back and forth
Nearly every day
And I hardly dream of hearing
A single compliment
Between the both of you.

You wouldn't be so harsh
With a stranger
So what makes you think
You can say such terrible things
To the people who are closer to you?
Wouldn't such a bit
Sting that much more
Coming from the people
Who *should* care more than a stranger?

I'm still shaking my head
And smiling
At your ignorance
After all
I wouldn't enjoy such cruel things.

Doesn't Mean

Maybe I write
About darker things
More than happy things
Because I don't need
To get the happy things out of me.

My writing
Takes my emotion
And puts it on a page
Sorts it out
Gives words color
Gives me a chance to heal

You may look
And see all the darkness I've written of
But that doesn't mean I'm not happy.

Miracle

Don't you realize
How glorious this day is?

Has it ever occurred to you
What miracles we're made of?

Have you ever thought about
How much beauty this world possesses?

The fact that we breathe
And our blood flows
That we have minds of our own
And flexible emotions
Every step we take
Is such a miracle!
Think!—
You have a foot!
Move your toes!
You only have to think
And it simply happens!

What blessed miracles
We are!

Still Yours.

I don't let anyone else
Talk to me the way you do
I don't know why
I would ever let you
But for some reason
I seem to be making excuses.

Well I just can't do that anymore
Can I?
No
Your words are still yours
No matter where they came from
Or why they came
It's still your decision
And I need to hold you up to that.

Filled

I almost let you
Cast me under such a dark spell
So dark
That even you
Couldn't see but a dim light!

How deep this tunnel!
How narrow this pit!
How cold these reckless waves!
How grey this confusion!
How heated is your anger!
How enduring is your hatred!
How unforgiving is your glare!

All this
–You so call it—love,
And yet you are still
So full of anger!

My dear
But how little you have grown!

Changing

You know, we see people
Online
Who we think are going to change the world
And make a difference.

But the real people
Who are going to make a real difference
Are never online
Because they're out in the real world
Making a real difference
And don't waste their time
Posting about it.

Your Love

Your love is very potent
Highly concentrated
I have never seen
Anything quite like it before.

It's no wonder I fell
I might've been the first
But I certainly won't be the last.

How foggy your mind must be
And I'm over in the clear

But ah
How desperately I love fog.

Gave In

There was a point
When I finally gave in.
Finally
I just dipped back
And began to drown

And even now
Just the memory
Of that place
Chills me to my bones
That horrifying
Dark
Frozen
Place

It was hardly escapable
And even now
My nerves jump at that thought
And my legs are ready to run
From that cold depression
Easily the worst I've ever been through

And the one I almost
Died trying to get out of.

Burden

My life has become
Horrifying scarlet!
How can I bear this pain
Any longer!

Where my dreams are of
Small children
Crying in dark corners
Though their burdens are heavy
I wish mine were as light as theirs!

And how I wish
I could just crumple up and sob
For so many days
But the result would be
Terrifyingly horrid

And so this pain
Wells up inside me
And I am left with
Such darkened thoughts
Seeing as I cannot cry!

Reputation

All I wish to do
Is cry!
I am not even allowed
This one satisfaction!
This one human response
Is restricted from me!

And for what!
For his reputation?
For all his lies
To be seen as truth?

I don't even need to state my opinion!
The facts of what he's done
Is enough to satisfy me

And so what must that say
Of his precious lies?

Not a Single Word

Think of it!
I am not even allowed
To properly defend myself
I am not even allowed
To properly speak!

This fire rages inside me
While the frost spreads over my mind
And not a word of it!
Not a single word
Uttered aloud

And do you realize why
All my words
Are written on this paper?
I cannot speak them
Nor express
How horrid this situation
Truly is!

Sorry Statement

Oh my darling!
What a sorry statement that is!
How insulting
That you should think me
That close minded

How insulting
That you should be so uncompassionate
How insulting
Is the way you speak of other people
How insulting
Is the way you speak of me

And don't you notice
The ludicrous words
That slip past your lips?
Of course not!
And do you not realize
How foolish you sound
Compared to me?
No! How should I have ever expected it!

Darling,
You have indeed surprised me.
And what a dark shock it is

Fate That Awaits You

I have done much
But if I am seen
As innocent
In everyone else's eyes
How much have you done?

If you have truly surpassed me
In wrongdoings
I am simply horrified
At the fate that awaits you

What a horrible
Future that is.
What magnificent consequences
What terrible frustration lies ahead

Oh, my dear children!
How could your minds be so twisted?
How could your hearts
Bear to grip the weight of your sins?

Glimpsed

It's like I'm only listening to
My first impression of you
I only wish to see
Your knowledge
And beauty
And humor.

However I now believe
My second impression is more accurate.
Unfortunately I had forgotten
All your cruel words
And stubbornness
Unforgiving glares
Harsh judgments.

I believe at this point
The cons outweigh the pros
I'm still struggling to see
But at least I have glimpsed them now.

Robbed

Isn't it odd
That the love you hold for each other
Robs everyone else?

Shouldn't love give?
And spread?

That's how I know
You don't really love each other
That facade you hold
With each other
Will only bring you down
Along with everyone around you.

I'm not afraid of you
No, certainly not
I'm afraid for your future
And that's why I must maintain my distance

Once Again

Well certainly
They do enjoy my company
Much more than yours.
And I'm certain you know why.

All of your insults
And snapping words
You know the results
—Oh I *know* you do
And still you speak of
Such cruel things.

You're not even trying
As hard as I am.
You're not trying
To turn things around for yourself
You'd rather sit there
In misery
And once again—
I will not join you.

Desert

You are one of my only demons
I'm sure that without
The thought of you
I would be much happier

Your darkness
How tempting it is
My eyes must desert from you.

Afraid! Ha!
How right you are!
Indeed I am afraid of you
But not of your power, no
I'm afraid of your weakness
I'm afraid of my willingness
To try and help you
When I cannot save you.

Last Laugh

I will always have the last laugh
Because I won't be there to hear yours.

Everytime you speak
All I hear are your foolish words
All I see is a drunken mind
You've drowned yourself
In so many insults
That now it's the only language you know.

I can see every time
That you try to manipulate me
Because you think I still care
You are so certain
That I still care
That you let no other possibility
Enter your mind

Is it that you still want me to care?
After all that time
Of trying to make me turn away
And now you miss my unconditional love?

I will always have the last laugh
Because I won't be there to hear yours

Such a Pest

Don't you realize
How stupid you sound?
How spiteful you are?
Your foolish words
Your foolish silence
A fool.
Indeed that's what you portray
To the people around you.

You are so cruel
You don't even try to hide it
It's not something to be proud of
Yet still I see no change coming.

Cruelty
Will get you nowhere in this life
What a fool you are
To hang on to such unkind remarks

And you wonder why
I avoid you so
I refuse to be seen
With such a pest.
I will not stand for your foolishness.

See The Day

See and that's what people don't get
Being smart
Isn't a luxury
It's a requirement of survival.
That's what abuse does to you

If you're not strong enough
It can mess you up
For your entire life

And that's why I don't appreciate
People commenting
On how smart I am
Because no one understands
That I have to do this
So that I can see the day
I make it out of this miserable hell hole

So Many Years

What a terrible thing
To live with such hatred
For so many years

I don't see how
Such raw fury
Could live for so many years

Oh how miserable
These next few years
Will be for you!

And ah,
But how happy I will be.

Felt

All this time
Of course I knew
That I was wanted
But I've never felt it
Quite this way before

This belonging feeling
It's so pure
So innocent
And oh!
But how hopeful!

One Category

You are a confusing subject
In my mind
I can't quite place you
In any one category

I quite ardently avoid you
Yet at the same time
You seem so magnetic

I flinch away from your cruel words
Yet at the same time
I long for your good ones

I push away the thought of you
Yet at the same time
I sit here writing of you.

Never Humble

Oh you fools!
You do not know me
How could I have hoped that you would?

Ah what a fool I am
For believing in you!
How could I think you deserved
Any ounce of my trust?

And yet it was thrown away!
You hold such ignorance
In the pit of your heart
You have become so proud
As to never humble yourselves
Unto knowledge.

Scoff

Oh and to never be known
That is my fate with you
To never be understood
Your blindness
What a wretched fool you are

Your understanding
How crippled it has become!
For I do believe
That at one point
You knew what you were doing
But how malnourished you've left your minds!

I wish you would leave me be
What a filthy pest your ignorance is
I can't help but scoff
At your blindness

Given Up

I've given up on you
No other way to put it
Hands thrown in the air
Eyes rolled
Feet turned
Ready to walk away
Disgusted at your rudeness
Fed up with your crudeness
Done with your thoughtlessness
Finished with your unhappiness

If you would just listen
For only a moment
You would understand
The nature of my surrender
And yet your blabbering tongue
Remains too loud for you to hear me

And I have learned
Through all my respect and patience
That your opinion
Is still most important to you
And that you wouldn't care if I left.

Defeated

As you can see
My energy is depleted
And why should I remain
Fighting you so?

I don't need to stand against you
This isn't my battle
Your past ways
Are clashing with your future
And I have nothing to do with you

God knows my intentions
God knows what lies you speak
God has already defeated the devil
And I don't need to stand here fighting you.

No Longer

I can see your misery
And I know you can see it
Still I don't understand
Why you leave it so.

It courses through your blood
Staining your thoughts
You know you don't like it
Still you do nothing o fix it

I'll no longer sit here
With all your unhappiness
I've tried to show you the way
But if you keep turning from me
There's not much I can do

Your blindness
Your deafness
I know you can see me
I know you can hear me

But I'll fight your misery no longer.

Unfamiliar

Ha!
Are you really so unfamiliar
With happiness
And utter gratitude
That you would call mine odd?

And I wondered why
I still walked with you
And now I know the reason
For my uncertainty!
You are so miserable
So untrusting
So rude
And so ignorant
As to see my happiness as strange!

Oh now I must really laugh!
At myself
At how stupid I was
To think I could be happy with you!

Your Jealousy

Your jealousy
How humorous that is!
You thought you had everything
But now you've glimpsed my happiness
And realized how miserable you were!

Your jealousy
At my light
You didn't attempt to banish your own darkness
No, you decided to try and spread it
And how unsuccessful you were!

Your jealousy
At my strength
And you regret your weakness
I've worked too hard
To sink to your low level

Your jealousy
At my knowledge
You didn't try to learn, no
And now your spit
Has mixed with your terrible pride.

Not On You

Oh but my dear
The stars are winking down on me
Aren't they?

I'm sorry to say
All I see in your life
Is dark fog
—A mist of confusion—
Crumbling buildings
—A terrible fall—
Shivering cold
—A chilled night—
With no warmth
To sustain you through it all.

Something About You

There's something about you
That makes me weak
So utterly indecisive
I don't even have anything to say to you
I would just stare and ponder

There's something about you
That is so wrong
So wrong
I want to just twist my hand in
And fix your life

You had always thought me disgusting
Is it because you see it so in yourself?
After all
That's the case with most of your words.

What happened to you?
I can feel that your past is twisted
But I can't quite see the knots
No—in fact,
Even you have have closed your eyes to it.

I dread your future
I can see the confusion
and pain

What terrible pain!

And at present
I sense you are more confused than ever
What a trial you face
Oh and there's something in me
That flinches from all of you

And yet still holds my gaze

Fleeting Second

There's something so beautiful
About your darkness
Oh and how demented
My dear,
Your resolve is as mist
I can feel as you waver

Too many days in the dark
And the light
Blinds you with denial
Oh and I laugh when our eyes meet!
When you do not remember if I am good or bad!
When for but a moment
You see my friendly intentions

When the darkness in your mind
Cannot comprehend new light
When you see the change in me
And see your own spite
The regret and absorption

And only a fleeting second
But how I have learned of you!

Deep Awareness

Half amused
And deeply concerned
We can't help but look

Oh and the memories
I see they haunt you
As well as they do me

Oh and I feel you
The glimpses I get of your thoughts
Are enough to show me how confused you are

What a deep awareness
That has developed
If reading minds was ever possible.

Carve

You carve your own death
With every step
And the blood that trails behind you
Has not always been your own

And hate will bring you nowhere
Save a rotted heart,
A rotted hell

You've wasted your time
On such selfish determination

Determination to put me down
Determination to not be wrong
But then again—
You have no hope of being right.

Unenlightened

No longer will I wear this confused expression
For I am certain
Yes quite certain
Certain
That it would be in my best interest
To keep away from you

So while I may be in turmoil
Over a decision
I will not let you see that
For you do not deserve it
You only deserve to see
My strength against you

No,
You don't get ot see me as I really am
Anymore
You had your chance
To share my happiness
And so now you will live unenlightened.

Menacing Snarl

Because I flinch when I see you
And I wish I could snarl
A blood red menacing
Twisted smile
What a staticy cackle I would bear
And the glistening fangs
Oh what satisfaction

I would snarl at you
I want you
Gone gone
Gone
Gone
Gone.
And her
gonegonegonegonegone

Leave already
go
And I sit here and snarl
As I flinch away from the thought of you

Why Should I?

I am a wild,
Startled animal
Why should I stay near you?
Why should I hesitate from fleeing?
Hesitate from freedom?

And you want me to care!
Or it should seem that way,
And maybe I still do.
After all
You can't convince anyone that I'm bad
And don't good people care?

Winter

The flakes
Brilliantly bright
Floating and drifting
Gently through the sky
Crossing paths
With pale rays of sunlight

Large mounds of
Fresh cool powder
Forming everywhere

Crisp, thin air
Holding tendrils
Of steamy breath
That slide through our lips

The world adapting
Into something so cold and beautiful

You Are Neither

I quickly became
More depressed
Until I really was
On the brink of death

Of course I'm afraid of you
Of course I don't look at you
You are my downtrodden mind
You are my entrapped spirit

I flinch from you
I scream inwardly
My frightened animal mind
My fresh raw heart

It begs to be safe
It begs to be happy
My dear you are neither
And what a horror it is!

Wouldn't Mind

I'm still not sure
What to think
At the same time
I am scared of both you
And what I found
I was capable of.

If you asked my opinion
Of how everything went down
I would not reply
For my opinion is silent
Undertain
Dark
Depressed
Easily broken
Easily shaken

I still don't know
What to think

I wouldn't mind
Never knowing

Didn't Know

It's like I didn't know
What sadness was before

No, not truly
I had known its
Mediocre child

But now tears
Are all too real to me
And your death
Is stone upon my memory

Don't Have To

Sometimes I wonder
If I really am crazy
As you like to say.
I certainly feel so.

I could be more sane
than the rest of you
It does seem likely

And still it makes sense
That I be mad
I do play the part quite often

But we both know
You don't have to act.

Floating Away

I can't even begin to describe
What you did to me
How insanely
Out of my brain
Everything felt
After you came in contact with me

The drowning
The drowning
My lungs filled with water
And I did not notice
For you were my oxygen

But air
In water
Does not stay.
All you were ever good for
Was floating away.

December 25, 2016

I hate him
I wish he were dead
No, no
Not dead
I wish he were in my clutches
With no one to stop me
From torturing him

He deserves nothing less
Than the absolute absence of mercy
I want to inflict on him
Countless years of emotional agony
Having him gone.
Is no longer enough.

To suffer a lifetime of suffering
What a fitting punishment
From all the people he's met

I want to tear his skin with my nails
I want to see him *bleed*
I want to hear his scream
Hear him cry out in pain
Hear his bones snap
I want to watch as bruises blossom
And tears stream down

He will be at my mercy
He will die under my fist

Destructive

Yes,
I loved you.
But what a destructive love it was.

It was
Fire fire fire
Everyday
And I loved the heat
I loved the lick of pain
That came with
Having to reject you
I always wanted
What I could not have.

I could just
Soak my brain in it
Forget about life
For a few months
Forget anything existed
Outside of you

I didn't even wish
For a love in which I could
Keep my head together
Keep my heart from falling to pieces
And though I don't deserve it

I still get to have it now.

You Choose

Touch the lives
Of the people around you
Reach out with a smile
And fingers spread
A welcoming grasp

Leave them
With an inspired mind
Full of admiration
Live your life
Like you're trying to impress someone

You choose solitude
You choose sadness
You choose confinement
Will your walls be built of stone
Or will they be light as air?

How Sick I Was

I'm battling for every breath
Battling for every next moment

When I
Could no longer turn to you
I thought the fight was over.
Thought my spark would die.
I didn't even really mind.
That's how sick I was
I gave up so easily
My brain gave up on instinct
The instinct to live
To fight
Had simply evaporated

I finally realized
I can't turn to anyone
Can't trust anyone to be there
No one was an option
Besides Him.

Found

Why should I be near you?
After I have found
The world to be so kind?

How should I ever dream of
Walking back to your cruel words?

Irreplaceable

You're irreplaceable
And I should be glad
I would never want
To meet another one of you
Another nightmare
For me to travel through

What a blessing
To be free of you
And never needing to turn back to
The disappointment
THat we could never
Truly be just friends.

Cling

I clench my fists
In silent fury
I laugh aloud
Though I know it is foolish

I tell myself
You're wrong
You're wrong
But most of the world
Would not agree
WIth what I know is right

I cling to my logic
I cling to my sanity
I cling to my denial
But it doesn't make me smile

The snarl grows
Wide with my envy
I shut you out
Shut you out of my mind
Your empty words
Your empty blushes
I see right past it
Still my eyes betray me so!

Hollow

Some days I feel so invincible from you
So free from you
And the smile never parts from my lips
My pleasure comes
In stoic bursts of laughter
I feel so angelic!
What a word—
Angelic!

Still others
My dagger thrusts towards you
I give you too much hate
Too much
Undeserved attention
I don't know why I watch
But as I watch you
The frost grows stronger!
Freezing my frown
No escaping the grey fog veil
A hollow pit at my center
A hollow pit in my mind—

I thought I was free of you!

Flooding

The monumental strength
I must maintain
To keep my wall of memories
From flooding back in

I grunt and thrust
a constant war
no victory
My temper grows
The fire within me

Cold water drains
The life out of sparks
Just like mine

Horror Movie

You are a horror movie,
My dear,
The same kind of fear
The same kind of scream
The same eyes widening
The shock waves through my stomach

The whole time
I'd never guessed
The truth of my terror

Not Bound

It would feel so good
To tear all this up
—My art—

To not be bound
By any word
Or page

To feel the fibers split
The sound ripping through the air
The chains of my past
Slowly burning
Into a freeing oblivion

To forget
Move past
Accept and advance
To never look back
Upon your face

But this is my art
This is my lesson
Part of who I am

The past may be dark
But that doesn't mean

That I can't face the sun

Destroy

I can feel the tear
Hear the rip
Soak in
Each fiber of freedom

The pages grasped in my hand
I tear until there are no strips
Only pieces left in my fist
The words torn in half

How freeing this is!
Why didn't I do it before?
To destroy my thoughts of you
Put an end to my pain

Dust

Our past is dust
There's no more you
There is only me
You'll never again
Be my priority

I will burn it up
Flames licking up the page
Lapping up my agony
Lavishing in my misery
I will bear it no more

A tightness in my chest
Has seemingly evaporated
One that I didn't know
Had even existed.
I will soon forget you.

Your Name

After months of you
Kicking down my esteem
It feels so good
To destroy your name

Every page
Contains some of your words
All of them cruel
All of them lies
I tore out the papers
One by one
I shredded them in my hands
The beautiful absence
Of your power

I felt each piece
WIthin my grasp
No longer will I read of you
Your words are torn in half
No longer will I seek you out
Your words are empty masks

The pain you caused me
I've shredded it up
It no longer exists
And I will learn to forget.

Found My Desire

I can feel it
In my soul
Finally I am free!
Not only am I rid of you!
I can feel this is
A cleansing day!

I want to be done
I want to be finished
This isn't just a step forward
I have found my desire
To move past you!

Found my desire
To be whole again
Found my desire
To abandon my brokenness
My sadness
Found my desire
To turn toward the light
And never peer into darkness again!

Knowing

A beautiful bed
Of torn up paper
I can finally rest
Knowing you are gone

www.ingramcontent.com/pod-product-compliance
Lightning Source LLC
Chambersburg PA
CBHW030355130626
46549CB00004B/1509